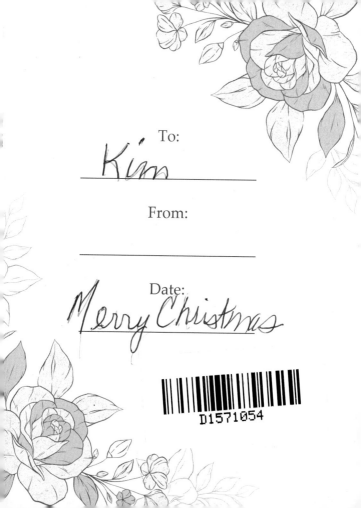

To:

Kim

From:

Date:

Merry Christmas

D1571054

Visit Christian Art Gifts website at www.christianartgifts.com.

Grace for Today

© 2022 Christian Art Publishers, RSA
        Christian Art Gifts Inc., IL, USA

Designed by Christian Art Gifts

Devotions written by Solly Ozrovech

Images used under license from Shutterstock.com

Printed in China

ISBN 978-1-63952-057-2

22 23 24 25 26 27 28 29 30 31 — 11 10 9 8 7 6 5 4 3 2

ONE-MINUTE DEVOTIONS®

grace
FOR TODAY

Carolyn Larsen

Christian art gifts®

january

CELEBRATING LIFE

Live Life to the Full

For with You is the fountain of life;
in Your light we see light.

PSALM 36:9

Life is the best thing God has given to you. So be grateful for it. When you accept the goodness of life, you will stop fighting against it.

When you accept that life is good, all impatience and frustration will be removed and life becomes a satisfying and exciting experience.

Allow your life to be controlled by godly principles and it will become an expression of those plans. You will possess a unity with the Creator, and your life will be filled with the fullness of God.

Creator God, I thank You that You have a plan for my life that is filled with the fullness of You. Amen.

Where Are You Heading?

Thanks be to God, who always leads
us in triumphal procession in Christ.

2 CORINTHIANS 2:14

It is not always easy to choose which road you should follow. But accepting Christ as Lord of your life puts divine powers into action. Your values in Him will provide you with an inspired yet practical goal.

Choosing your goal and objectives with Christ will put you on the right road and will bring joy, confidence and enthusiasm into your life.

If you walk through life in the light of God, the whole journey becomes a joyous experience.

*Dear Guide, thank You that I can walk through
life with You and that You guide me
along the paths of life. Amen.*

A New Year with God

"I will instruct you and teach you in the way you should go; I will counsel you and watch over you."

PSALM 32:8

The prospect of a new year can be exciting because of many new possibilities and opportunities, but also disquieting if you face the future with anxiety – wondering whether the problems and disasters of the past will repeat themselves.

International crises, financial setbacks, as well as personal problems and disappointments tend to cloud our vision of the future.

Always remember that you can place your hope in the omniscience of God. He truly cares about you and He loves you deeply. Believe in the promises of Jesus and approach the new year in His loving presence. He will guide you through the labyrinth of life because He knows what is best for you.

You are truly a God of love! Thank You for sending Your only Son so that I, too, can be saved. Amen.

Something to Live For

"Before long, the world will not see Me anymore,
but you will see Me. Because I live, you also will live."

JOHN 14:19

Many people harbor anxiety because the future is unknown to them, and become pessimistic and discouraged. We must constantly remind ourselves that life is extremely precious, so that we don't fall into the trap of depression.

Even if the future seems bleak, you can be assured that your life and future are in God's hands. God is in control of everything. There is joy in Christ because He is the Rock on which you can build your life. His grace is sufficient to get you through each day.

Seize this life and live it in the abundance of Jesus Christ your Lord and Savior.

*Through all the changing circumstances of life, Lord,
in joy as well as sorrow, my heart will sing
Your praises and thank You for the abundant life
that You have made possible for me. Amen.*

An Open Door

"See, I have placed before you an
open door that no one can shut."

REVELATION 3:8

Constant grumbling makes life seem meaningless. It doesn't take someone who lives like this
long to develop a negative, cynical attitude towards life.

But Christ wants so much more for us. Scripture, history and personal experience all offer
ample testimony to the fact that an ordinary,
seemingly meaningless life can be transformed
by the power of the living Christ and through
His Holy Spirit.

This new life of abundance that Christ offers
you is yours for the taking. Turn to Christ and
He will open the door to a new, meaningful life
for you.

*Lord Jesus, the open door of Your grace leads me into
the abundance and joy of life in Your presence. Fill
my life with new purpose and meaning today. Amen.*

Experience Christ's Fullness

God was pleased to have all His fullness dwell in Him,
and through Him to reconcile to Himself all things.

COLOSSIANS 1:19–20

Jesus was not just "a good person," He was more than good. He was the personification of perfection.

This breathtaking truth is so overwhelming that we might even hesitate to approach the Lord. But, if He is your Savior, there is no barrier that can separate you from Him. Because of this, life becomes filled with fullness!

Ephesians 3:17-18 reads: "So that Christ may dwell in your hearts through faith. And I pray that you, being rooted and established in love, may have power, together with all the saints, to grasp how wide and long and high and deep is the love of Christ."

How privileged we are, as God's children, to partake in His festival of love.

I praise and glorify You, O Loving Savior, that,
through faith, You abide in my heart.
Make it a worthy abode. Amen.

Life in All Its Fullness

*That you may be filled to the measure
of all the fullness of God.*

EPHESIANS 3:19

There are people who have lost interest in life and are filled with despair because of circumstances or negative dispositions.

Although setbacks, which shake the core of our very foundations, and disappointments are a part of life, we must never lose sight of Jesus. He came so that we may have abundant life. He promises to be with us in every situation; He promises to carry our burdens. All we need to do is turn to Him in faith.

Enter into an intimate relationship with the living Christ through prayer and meditation. Share your problems with Him, and you will experience profound joy and peace.

*Lord, You sprinkle Your blessings over me like
soft rain. You gladden my heart. Grant me
the fullness of Your Spirit. Amen.*

Positive Thinking

Be transformed by the renewing of your mind.
Then you will be able to test and approve what
God's will is – His good, pleasing and perfect will.

ROMANS 12:2

The teachings of our Lord embraces positive thinking, but it reaches beyond thoughts to touch the hidden possibilities of the spirit.

When we face the reality of situations in our lives, positive thinking can help up to a point, but a relationship with the living Christ can do so much more.

Positive thinking can only bring about limited solutions. Real change comes when you move past thinking, to an unshakable trust of God's work in your life.

Positive thinking, together with solid faith in the Almighty Christ, is a creative force that enables you to live as God intended you to live – in victory and with joy.

Holy Spirit, fill my heart with courage and the faith to know the good, perfect and pleasing will of God. Amen.

The Future Is Yours

*"I have come that they may have life,
and have it to the full."*

JOHN 10:10

Perhaps your past tells a story of frustration or you feel that your life is uninspired and dull, and that nothing you do is worthwhile.

But the future belongs to you; it is yours. Every day is a gift from the loving hand of God, and you can only live life to the full when you surrender to His purpose for your life.

Achieving your purpose in life depends on your relationship with Christ. If your life has a spiritual foundation, it must also have a spiritual goal. It is by acknowledging this truth and applying it in your own life that you are guaranteed complete deliverance, joy and fulfillment. Then you can utilize God's precious gift of living life to the full.

*Thank You that I can have everlasting life
through Christ's crucifixion. Not even
death can make me fear. Amen.*

Make Today Wonderful

This is the day the LORD has made;
let us rejoice and be glad in it.

PSALM 118:24

Regardless of how bad things appear, God is greater than any situation.

Every day is a unique gift to you from God. What you make of it is your responsibility. The way in which you welcome each new day will depend on your frame of mind and attitude towards life.

Fortunately, your frame of mind is not something that you have to leave in the hands of fate or coincidence. God has given you the ability to choose your frame of mind, as well as the pace of your life. Meet every day with joy and expectation, and then you can live a happy, victorious life!

Father, I experience the reality of Your presence every moment of the day. Teach me to number my days in such a way that I will become wise. Amen.

Appreciate Life

I will sacrifice a thank offering to You
and call on the name of the LORD.

PSALM 116:17

Do you appreciate the love and support of your family? Can you still marvel at the rising of the sun? Can you still laugh about a funny situation, or do you find it hard to believe that humor is one of God's gifts to you?

Don't let your enthusiasm for life wane! Enjoying and appreciating the beauty of life must be an integral part of your life.

If you put God at the center of your life and thoughts, you will discover that, by appreciating your life, you continually move closer to Him, the Source of all real life.

Father, I appreciate all the beauty and joy that fills my life and that You have so freely bestowed on me. Amen.

Be Transformed

He who pursues righteousness and
love finds life, prosperity and honor.

PROVERBS 21:21

The quality of your life depends on your attitude and the way in which you approach and plan your life.

In God's Word you will find numerous examples of people who had seemingly useless, unimportant lives, and yet they were transformed into inspired disciples through Jesus.

Christ specifically came that you may have life in abundance. Turn to Him and walk your life's path in the company of the living Christ; you will discover a new self-confidence and develop abilities that can only be received from the Holy Spirit.

Holy Spirit, I plead that You would help me to make decisions that lead to life and that bring joy. Amen.

Find Joy in the Small Things

Everything God created is good, and nothing is
to be rejected if it is received with thanksgiving.

1 TIMOTHY 4:4

Many of us tend to take things for granted – the colors of flowers, the songs of birds, the beauty of a sunrise – these are all things that many people barely notice.

It is only when you begin to contemplate a life without these blessings that you realize how colorless and uninteresting it would be if they were absent.

We should cherish and appreciate every blessing in our lives. We should learn to appreciate the wonders of God's Creation and everything He has granted us through His grace.

Heavenly Father, I thank You for the everyday things in my life and for what they mean to me. Amen.

Live Fully

We pray this in order that you may live a life
worthy of the Lord and may please Him in
every way: bearing fruit in every good work,
growing in the knowledge of God.

COLOSSIANS 1:10

People often seem to be bored or dissatisfied
with life. Every moment of Jesus' life on earth
was filled with purpose and meaning, and in
everything He did the will of the Father and
brought glory and honor to His name.

God expects you to follow in Jesus' footsteps – right here and now. Enter into His holy
presence often and allow Him to fill your life
with new purpose, new goals and new joy.

Let your attitude be the same as Jesus'. Fulfill His will and obey Him in all things and
your life will yield a rich harvest that will glorify God.

*Perfect Example and Redeemer, through You I can
rejoice in the blessed knowledge that I can experience
true life in all its richness and fullness. Amen.*

Reach Your Goals

Walk in His ways, and keep His decrees and
commands, His laws and requirements,
so that you may prosper in all you do.

1 KINGS 2:3

Few people can honestly say that success means nothing to them.

For those who have a passionate desire to succeed, failure can be a bitter pill to swallow. Many people lose confidence because they fear that they will never obtain success.

It is important to accept the fact that it is impossible to be successful through your own abilities. You need Jesus Christ's guidance and support to help you make the right decisions.

If the living Christ is your partner in life, then you can rest assured that everything you do will bring a deep and lasting sense of fulfillment.

Holy Spirit, please help me to stay on course
and to achieve success in all that You
have called me to do. Amen.

The Right Way

Walk in all the way that the LORD your God has
commanded you, so that you may live and prosper and
prolong your days in the land that you will possess.

DEUTERONOMY 5:33

Many people wonder if it is worthwhile trying to lead a good life. They maintain high standards of honesty, integrity and righteousness, yet they see others experiencing prosperity and success in spite of their dubious lives.

However, to ensure a life of peace and liberty for yourself you must always try to follow the example of Jesus Christ. In order to experience the abundant life which He offers, you need to live according to His prescriptions and follow His example.

This is the only way in which you will taste the joy and fulfillment that are the portion of those who walk along the way established by the living Guide.

*Lord Jesus, help me to follow Your
example and live a life of honesty, integrity,
righteousness, compassion and love. Amen.*

God Makes Life Good

Listen to this, Job; stop and consider God's wonders.

JOB 37:14

We live in troubled and uncertain times where basic values and integrity have been pushed aside. Sadly, many people have given up trying to promote a sense of morality and have chosen to just go with the flow.

If you are in this position, then, like Job, you should pause and consider God's wonders.

Reflect on the wonderful deeds of God. Out of chaos and darkness He created this beautiful earth. He loved us so much that He saved us from the bonds of sin and death. Through the life of Jesus He gave us an example of the fullness of life.

Praise Him for all His wonderful deeds and for His indescribable grace.

Lord, You fill my heart with gladness. Thank You for Your glorious deeds I see all around me every day. Amen.

Remember Who You Are

So God created man in His own image,
in the image of God He created him.

GENESIS 1:27

When it seems as if nothing in your life is working out, when loneliness takes hold of you and despondency descends upon you, it is time to remember a few spiritual facts.

You were created in the very image of God. You are a spiritual being with a rich spiritual heritage.

You do not need to be at the mercy of moods and emotions beyond your control. You have been created for spiritual greatness, and when you live in the awareness of God's presence, you will be fulfilled.

*My Savior, because of my spiritual heritage
and the awareness of Your living presence,
I can face life with confidence. Amen.*

Handle the Pressure with Jesus

Those who pursue us are at our heels;
we are weary and find no rest.

LAMENTATIONS 5:5

The extensive pressure of modern life causes tremendous tension. Insecurity about the future creates a sense of danger. The amount of tension that is built up, robs many lives of their sparkle and purposefulness. Thus people break down under the pressure and unbearable load of their fears and problems.

In order for you to live confidently in these demanding times, it is imperative that your life be dedicated to the living Christ. It is only through Him that all things become possible. It is through His guidance only that you will be able to live life to the full and be happy.

Make the Lord your guide and companion on your pilgrimage, and fears and worries will not have a paralyzing effect on your life.

Loving Guide, with You by my side
I know that anything is possible and
I can live a full, happy life. Amen.

Count Your Blessings

Whoever invokes a blessing in the
land will do so by the God of truth.

ISAIAH 65:16

To the optimist, the simple things in life are a constant source of joy – spontaneous laughter, the bright rays of the sun, and the sounds of the birds in the trees.

People who count their blessings are extremely happy. Even in their darkest moments they maintain a spirit of hope and optimism, because they know things will work out well.

The more you count your blessings, the more it will seem as if God pours them out upon your life. Your heart will overflow with gratitude for God's amazing love. When life becomes a burden and it seems ominously dark around you, recalling your blessings is a sure way to keep a healthy perspective.

Father, how will I ever be able to express my gratitude
in words? You bless me with so many things
that were I to start listing them one by one,
I would need eternity to thank You. Amen.

Spontaneous Thanksgiving

Your ways, O God, are holy. What god is so great as our God? You are the God who performs miracles; You display Your power among the peoples.

PSALM 77:13-14

We serve a wonderful God! Unfortunately we sometimes lose sight of His greatness and end up leading unfulfilled lives. Instead of growing into the fullness of His stature by focusing on Him, we try to reduce Him to our level.

God is great and Scripture resounds with His invitation for us to share in His greatness. Surrendering to His presence transforms dwarves into spiritual giants.

When you are aware of God living in you, your attitude to life changes and your heart will overflow with gratitude for the glory and beauty that God imparts to your daily life.

Wondrous God, because You dwell in me through Jesus Christ I can overcome all the negative things in life and be filled with all the goodness of Your Holy Spirit. Amen.

Set Free by the Holy Spirit

Where the Spirit of the Lord is, there is freedom.

2 CORINTHIANS 3:17

Have you ever felt that you are able to achieve more than you do presently and that you are not nearly reaching your full potential? You might be frustrated because of the monotonous routine of your life. You don't expect anything exciting to happen to you anymore.

When you allow the Holy Spirit to come into your life and take control, you can expect some radical changes. When the Spirit of God accompanies you, you will become aware of a certain pattern taking shape in your life. Suddenly there will be meaning and purpose in your life and you will be empowered by an indescribable feeling of real freedom.

Your traveling companion, the Holy Spirit, is not only your guide, but also the One who protects and inspires you!

Father, through the wisdom and power of the Holy Spirit, help me to realize my true purpose in life. Amen.

Days When Things Go Wrong

To whom do you belong, and where are you going, and who owns all these animals in front of you?

GENESIS 32:17

Life must have purpose and significance if you are to live meaningfully. One of the great truths of the Christian life is that it changes your attitude. Previously you lived without hope or expectation, but Christ now plants new hope in your heart.

When you truly start living in Christ, you look at life with new understanding. You will never again have to ask, "Is life worthwhile?" When the thoughts of Christ fill you and the Holy Spirit saturates your spirit, you realize the rich quality of your faith, and your life takes on new and exciting dimensions.

Lord Jesus, You came so that we may have abundant life. Help me to remember to come to You when days are dark, so that my life may be infused with significance and meaning once again. Amen.

Your Words
Are My Delight

When Your words came, I ate them; they were my joy and my heart's delight. Therefore this is what the Lord says: "If you repent, I will restore you that you may serve Me; if you utter worthy, not worthless, words, you will be My spokesman."

JEREMIAH 15:16, 19

In answer to his prayer, God told Jeremiah that he should speak words that have value. Words can be used for either positive or negative means. Think carefully about how your words can be used for good rather than evil. The prophet Jeremiah said to the Lord, "Your words were my joy and my heart's delight."

God's encouraging words helped him and supported him greatly during the persecution that he had to endure. God wants to help you too. Let your words before God always be positive and let His Word always be a joy in your prayer life.

Lord God, help me to always speak words that are worthy and that bring glory and honor to You. Amen.

God's Will Be Done

"My food," said Jesus, "is to do the will of Him
who sent Me, and to finish His work."

JOHN 4:34

In order for you to experience abundance, joy
and fulfillment in this new year you need to do
that which you believe is God's will for your
life. When your whole life is set on doing the
will of God, then you come to a full understanding of the real meaning and purpose of life.

You will know that it is your highest goal and
greatest joy to do the will of God. While you
dedicate yourself to achieve this objective, the
real purpose of your life will unfold before you.
While you practice to do the will of God, you
will discover that you have an inner strength
which results from obeying His will. Like the
living Christ you will also know by experience:
"My food is to do the will of Him who sent Me."

Father, my food is to do Your will for my life.
Guide me in understanding and obeying
Your will in every area of my life. Amen.

Seize the Day!

"In the time of My favor I heard you,
and in the day of salvation I helped you."

2 CORINTHIANS 6:2

When you look back on your life, there are certain highlights that tend to stand out – great moments in your life.

The truth is that every day could be a great day in your life if only you appreciated the present and passing moment. Every day is a new birth, with new prospects and opportunities that fall to you from the loving hand of God, so that you can live.

Cherish your memories, but appreciate the importance and wonderful possibilities of today. Accept every moment of every day as a gift of grace from the hand of God and utilize it fully. Then every day will be a great day.

*When I am confused and surrounded by darkness,
I know that You will deliver me. You are great
and good and do not scorn my feeble prayers.
Thank You for Your constant presence. Amen.*

The Road Ahead

"Have I not commanded you? Be strong
and courageous. Do not be terrified; do not
be discouraged, for the LORD your God
will be with you wherever you go."

JOSHUA 1:9

Many people try to discover the secrets of what
the future holds, but nobody really knows what's
in store for us.

Instead of fretting about the unknown, prepare yourself for any eventuality that God may
bring on your path. To be able to enter the unknown future in hope and trust, a positive and
living faith in God is imperative.

When Christ lives in your heart and in your
thoughts, you will be able to face the future
without fear. You will have the quiet assurance
that you will not be confronted by any situation that you and the living Christ will not be
able to overcome together.

*Lord, I rejoice in the knowledge that You hold my life
in Your hands. I trust You with my entire life. Amen.*

A Life of Happiness

I know that there is nothing better for men
than to be happy and do good while they live.

ECCLESIASTES 3:12

It is not a sin to be happy. Your heavenly Father gave you a life to be treasured and enjoyed to the full. If it is filled with the spice of laughter and humor, you are that much richer.

Live your life so that it is interspersed with joy and happiness. You have reason for great joy: God loves you, Christ died for you and the Holy Spirit leads you onto joyous paths.

The sublime peace of God is the main source of all true happiness. Make time to live life to the full, and with the help of the Holy Spirit develop a cheerful and positive outlook on life.

Lord, You are present in every phase of my life.
You comfort me in sorrow, but You also bless
me in abundance. With You by my side,
I will not be afraid of anything. Amen.

Purposefully into the Future

In all your ways acknowledge Him,
and He shall direct your paths.

PROVERBS 3:6 (NKJV)

An experience with the living Christ gives purpose and meaning to your life. People who exist without any purpose will never experience the joy of achievement and life-fulfillment.

Ambitious people know what they want and are willing to work hard to achieve that. The tragedy, however, occurs when, after they have achieved everything they set out to achieve, they still have the gnawing feeling that they have missed out on something important.

If you have disregarded the spiritual aspect of life, you probably missed the most important truth. God has bestowed upon you the gracious gift of life in order for you to serve Him.

Father God, thank You for the gracious gift
of life You have given me. Amen.

Assess Yourself

Do not think of yourself more highly than you ought.

ROMANS 12:3

Many people have a poor opinion of themselves and their abilities. Such people lead unhappy and frustrated lives, because that which you believe of yourself is inevitably reflected in your way of life.

As a Christian disciple, sooner or later you must assess yourself in the light of God's Holy Spirit. This could be a humbling experience or it could reveal a revelation, and you will begin to see who you can become through God's strength, wisdom and inspiration.

Stop disparaging yourself and convincing yourself that you will never achieve anything worthwhile. You were created in the image of God and in His eyes you are invaluable. If you embrace this truth, the honest assessment of your life is about to begin.

Jesus Christ, I am endlessly grateful
to have been redeemed by Your blood.
Through You I can inherit eternal life. Amen.

Lean on God

From the fullness of His grace we have
all received one blessing after another.

JOHN 1:16

Sometimes life and circumstances can get you down. If you are feeling depressed or pessimistic, it is up to you to refresh your spirit by entering into an intimate relationship with the living Christ through prayer and meditation.

Like a needy child, tell God about all your problems and concerns. Share your troubles and anxieties with Him. The Word says, "Cast all your anxiety on Him because He cares for you" (1 Pet. 5:7). Do this and you will experience joy and peace like only God can give.

Through God's immense grace you will find meaning and direction for your life, and your life will be crowned with the success of God.

Lord, thank You that because of Your unfailing love,
I have a reason to celebrate life no matter
what trials I'm going through. Amen.

february

KEEPING THE FAITH

The Lord Is Our Shepherd

The LORD is my shepherd, I shall not be in want.

PSALM 23:1

Those of us who belong to the Lord know we are safe and secure. We know for certain that the Lord is our Shepherd and therefore we do not fear the future because our Shepherd is already there. He will walk before us every day, leading us to our eternal destination.

Sometimes we have doubts about the future. We wonder whether we will have enough to provide for our essential needs. With childlike certainty, the psalmist then tells us, "I shall not be in want." You shall not be "in want" of anything that you truly need and that is good for you. The Lord will hear when you call, because His love never changes.

Lord God, it is a glorious reassurance to me that You are my Shepherd and that in Your hands I am safe and secure. Amen.

Spiritual Maturity

*You, however, are controlled not by the sinful nature
but by the Spirit, if the Spirit of God lives in you.*

ROMANS 8:9

The direction that your life has taken reveals where the emphasis in your life lies. You may achieve your material objectives, but is that enough? Is that why God gave you life?

Remember, you are also a spiritual being, therefore, your spirit can only ever be fully satisfied when it is in a dynamic relationship with the Holy Spirit.

This intimately personal relationship with God can only be attained by faith in the resurrected Christ; a faith that is more than a fleeting emotion; a faith that accepts His authority in all aspects of life. This type of faith will give true sense and meaning to your life.

*I never want to be separated from You, Lord. I wish
to experience Your love and be a fruitful vine in
Your kingdom. I want to glorify You. Amen.*

When Dark Clouds Gather

Surely God is my salvation; I will trust and not be
afraid. The Lord, the Lord, is my strength and
my song; He has become my salvation.

ISAIAH 12:2

It is a fact of life that sometimes storm clouds gather, darkening our lives, and it is futile to ignore them, hoping they will disappear.

Instead, stand firm with a living faith in the Almighty God, who controls the storms and hurricanes.

However threatening the circumstances of life may be, it is imperative that you do not allow anything to take God's central role in your life. With Him as the center you will maintain your balance. The ominous clouds might still be present, but you will be assured that your loving Father is working everything together for your good.

Even when everything around me is
shrouded in darkness, You will
shield me. Thank You, Father. Amen.

Get the Most from Your Faith

"Whoever has will be given more. Whoever does not have, even what he has will be taken from him."

MATTHEW 13:12

Unfortunately, there are people who have never been inspired to walk intimately with the Lord. As a result of this, their faith is weak and their discipleship is ineffectual.

The world needs disciplined Christians to affirm and proclaim the teachings of Jesus, particularly His command, "As I have loved you, so you must love one another" (John 13:34).

The discipline that is needed to live a life of Christian love demands a strength that can only come from the Holy Spirit. This is nurtured through prayer, Bible study and a hunger for a more profound experience with God.

I plead with You, O Jesus, for the gift of Your Holy Spirit so that my faith can be fully experienced. Amen.

Faith Is a Process of Growth

Grow in the grace and knowledge of our
Lord and Savior Jesus Christ.

2 PETER 3:18

It is sad that many Christians make little progress in their spiritual lives after accepting Christ as their Savior.

Ask yourself this: Is Christ becoming more real to me? Is prayer essential in my decision-making? Do I find God's will for my life in the Scriptures? Am I nearer to Christ than I was when I was born again?

It takes courage to answer these questions. Allow this to be a prelude to renewing your faith in Christ and there will be no end to the growth and development it will bring forth. This growth will bring life-giving energy, enabling you to develop in Christlikeness and bear fruit in God's kingdom.

You are the true Vine, Lord. Keep me from evil and help me to be truly fruitful in You. Amen.

A Most Enriching Experience

"Remain in Me, and I will remain in you."

JOHN 15:4

It is worth remembering that the stars are still shining, even when clouds hide them. Remember, too, that behind the dark patches of life, the eternal love of your heavenly Father is still shining brightly. If you have cultivated trust in Him, your faith will carry you through the darkest moments of life.

The life that Jesus promises us if we "remain in Him" is such a challenge that people hesitate to accept it and instead choose to remain in a religious rut that promotes neither joy nor spiritual growth.

The life that Christ promises is much more than an emotional experience. It creates inner peace, a constructive purpose in life, and provides the strength to achieve and maintain such a life through the power of the Holy Spirit.

Holy Father, I praise and glorify You for the life-changing strength that flows from Christ. Amen.

God Is in Control

Job replied to the Lord: "I know that You can
do all things; no plan of Yours can be thwarted."

JOB 42:1-2

Everywhere you go you will meet pessimistic
people – people who see no hope and carry an
atmosphere of gloom around with them.

Rather than give in to despair, consider the
greatness of God. Look back over the years and
you will find many examples of the wonderful ways in which God transforms despair into
hope; sorrow into joy; and defeat into victory.

When things around you appear dark and
terrifying, hold onto the promises of God. Remember His mighty deeds, and continue in confidence and with the certain knowledge that He
is wholly in control.

Almighty God and loving Father, my heart's knowledge
that You are in control allows me to be courageous
even in dark days. Guide me on Your path
and keep my faith strong. Amen.

Grow in Faith

Immediately the boy's father exclaimed,
"I do believe; help me overcome my unbelief!"

MARK 9:24

Many Christians urge fellow believers to, "Just believe!" but it's not always that easy, especially when the storm clouds close in around you.

Fortunately, through the grace of God it is easy to develop a mature and sincere faith. Recall an incident in your life when something out of the ordinary happened and thank God for it. It might not be something big or significant, but when you recall the incident, it strengthens your faith in a wonderful way.

Make a habit of remembering small answers to prayer, and your faith will gradually grow to the extent where you will receive bigger revelations from God.

Loving Master, I want to grow in my faith so that I can bring glory and honor to You in everything I do and say. Amen.

Believing without Seeing

Therefore we are always confident.
We live by faith, not by sight.

2 CORINTHIANS 5:6-7

When you are facing problems, difficulties or tough decisions, do you trust God sufficiently to put yourself and your future in His hands?

Jesus came to confirm that God loves you unconditionally. His care, help and compassion are unquestionable. You are precious in His sight. Therefore, Christ will not allow anything to harm you.

With this assurance, you can trust God unconditionally in everything. Then you will walk along His path, doing His will.

If you do this, you will experience peace and tranquility of mind. Even if you cannot see the complete road ahead, faith will carry you through.

Lord, please be with me in the dark days, and
shine the light of Your presence before
me so that I do not stumble. Amen.

Trust in God

As for me, I watch in hope for the LORD, I wait
for God my Savior; my God will hear me.

MICAH 7:7

Some people look at the stars or consult for-
tune-tellers in order to "see" their future.

However trustworthy these methods seem,
they cannot help us handle the unknown. The
only way in which we can be filled with confidence about the future is by believing in God.

When you are facing a problem and doubt
tries to take hold of you, this is when Jesus comes
to you, saying, "Take courage! It is I. Don't be
afraid" (Matt. 14:27). Christ Himself will bring
you peace of mind.

*Loving Savior, I place myself completely under
Your control, for I know that You alone can
guarantee me peace of mind. Amen.*

Do You Truly Believe?

Be strong and take heart, all you who hope in the LORD.

PSALM 31:24

How solid is your faith? Have you reduced it to outward matters of attending church, singing songs of praise, listening to nice sermons and trying to live a respectable life?

Your faith only becomes reality when the external ceremonies of Christianity become a pulsating and powerful experience in your soul. It becomes a reality when you no longer see yourself as someone defeated by sin because God's Holy Spirit, who resides in you, enables you to triumph over all sin.

You must develop the discipline of experiencing Christ's presence in your everyday life. Prayer, Bible study and fellowship with other believers are essential to attaining a positive, living and dynamic faith.

Lord, You are my only shelter. When I feel powerless and afraid, You will lead me through the darkness and give me renewed courage. Amen.

The Light on Your Way

God said, "Let there be light," and there was light.

GENESIS 1:3

When we look back along the road we have traveled, we tend to focus only on the negative things. Because the past had its share of problems, many people expect the same from the future.

But this is a negative way of looking at life. The prayer of your heart every day should be, "Lead me, O Light of the world!" Jesus Christ is still the Light of the world and He has promised that those who follow Him will never walk in darkness. Take His hand in faith and trust and experience Him as the light of your life.

God of light and truth, thank You that Your Son has illuminated my life so that I can walk into the future in faith and trust. Be my light, even when darkness falls around me. Amen.

God Remains in Control

He is before all things, and in Him
all things hold together.

COLOSSIANS 1:17

There are times when it seems as if everything is going wrong. Throughout history, people have struggled through disasters, hardships, dangers, sorrow and adversity.

Before becoming despondent, however, acknowledge the greatness, glory and constancy of God. He called the world into existence and has kept vigil over His creation, caring for us through the ages and sheltering us in every disaster.

He is the Creator God who will never abandon us. Hold onto His promises; place your entire trust and faith in the living Christ and through Him you will survive all dangers and adversities.

You are eternal, Lord, and the workmanship of Your Creation bears testimony to Your great glory. Amen.

Blessed Assurance

Commit to the LORD whatever you do,
and your plans will succeed.

PROVERBS 16:3

Planning is important in every area of life. You plan for the future, for your marriage, for your finances and for retirement. Much of our time and energy goes into planning.

There is a way to make planning better, however, but it requires strict spiritual discipline to make it effective and it must be undertaken with sincerity and honesty. It also requires solid faith and trust in God and in His promises.

Whatever your concern may be, lay it before God in prayer with all your fears and expectations, trusting Him completely.

Leave the matter in God's hands. In His own perfect time and way, He will show you how to bring it to pass.

Dear Lord, guide me to follow Your commands
and to fulfill Your will in obedience. Amen.

Faith That Counts

*The only thing that counts is faith
expressing itself through love.*

GALATIANS 5:6

People have different opinions regarding what is most important in our spiritual lives.

Your faith will be ineffective if it does not lead you to a more profound knowledge and awareness of God.

Faith is alive when it is expressed through love. Without love, faith becomes dead and the height, depth and eternal nature of God's love cannot be experienced. If you possess a living faith, manifested in love, you have the basic qualities of a practical, inspired and effective religion that is acceptable to God.

*Lord, Your Word teaches me to love You with
my whole heart, soul and mind, and to love
my neighbor as myself. Grant me the strength
to abide by these commandments. Amen.*

God Has a Plan for You

Do not be distressed and do not be angry with
yourselves for selling me here, because it was
to save lives that God sent me ahead of you.

GENESIS 45:5

It is often difficult to understand that God is fulfilling His plan in your life, especially when times
are tough. When Joseph was sold into slavery, he
probably struggled to discern God's will. Nevertheless, many years later, he recognized that God
had been with him through it all.

God determines the pattern of your life. In your
present circumstances, difficult as they might be,
hold on to the assurance that God is busy working
out His perfect plan for your life. Life's darkest
moments can become a testimony of God's perfect purpose for your life.

*Faithful Guide, I will trust You to lead me surely
along the pathways through life, even when
the dark shadows hide my way. Amen.*

Conquer Depression

"For you who revere My name, the sun of righteousness will rise with healing in its wings."

MALACHI 4:2

Depression and pessimism are ailments that can destroy a person's soul. Apart from the fact that depression is an illness of the mind, it also affects your physical and spiritual well-being, limits your vision of the future, and negatively influences your attitude towards life.

The only way to fight such an emotional disruption effectively is to turn to Christ and open yourself to His love and healing.

Place yourself unconditionally in His care. When Jesus guides you along the path you need to take through life, you will find that because of your obedience to Him, you will be filled with a sense of self-confidence and well-being that only He can give you.

I cling to You, Lord Jesus, in the knowledge that nothing in this life can harm me as long as You are with me. Amen.

Comfort in the Word

*Open my eyes that I may see
wonderful things in Your law.*

PSALM 119:18

Disillusionment and dejection are common among people who have developed a negative outlook on life.

In order to live and not merely exist, it is essential to nurture a positive attitude – even when things are not going well. Your faith will need to be strong if you are to triumph over your problems with joy.

Scripture is filled with stories of how ordinary people, like you and me, overcame hostile forces in the name of the Lord. Draw comfort from the Word and through Jesus Christ, the incarnate Word. Then you will be able to triumph over any adversity.

You reveal Yourself in Your Word. It is trustworthy, steadfast and unfailing. Thank You that I can know the abundant life that is found in Your Word. Amen.

God's Love Endures Forever

Though I walk in the midst of trouble, You preserve my life. The Lord will fulfill His purpose for me; Your love, O Lord, endures forever – do not abandon the works of Your hands.

PSALM 138:7–8

You might sometimes feel that God has abandoned you when you needed Him most. But through faith you need to hold fast to what you know is true about God, even when you cannot see any results.

Although we are inclined to plan our whole course through life, we can confess, together with David, "The Lord will fulfill His purpose for me." In the time of his worst trial, David still trusted God to protect him. Be assured that the Lord will never neglect the work of His hands, so even in the dark times, remember that God is faithful and you can never drift too far away from the sphere of His love.

Loving God, protect me from the anger of my enemies. Thank You that there is no end to Your love. Amen.

Find Strength in God

O Lord, be gracious to us; we long for You. Be our strength every morning, our salvation in time of distress.

ISAIAH 33:2

Immediately after praying to God to save Israel, Isaiah describes Israel's distress: the Assyrians rejected their petition for peace, Lebanon was destroyed, and the plains of Sharon resembled a wilderness.

Isaiah's trust in God never faltered. He believed God's promises that He would preserve Israel and deliver His people. Because of this Isaiah could pray with confidence, "Be our strength every morning, our salvation in times of distress."

Like Isaiah, we can depend on God in times of distress and trouble. Call on Him in such times and feel the strength, that can only come from God, descend on you.

Omnipotent and omniscient God, help me to trust in Your promises. Be my strength and my salvation each day. Amen.

Equipped through Faith

When I sit in darkness, the Lord will be a light to me.

MICAH 7:8 (NKJV)

In order to survive in trying times, it is extremely important that your faith in the risen Christ be powerful. Dark times are in actual fact the very times during which you must be able to look back and see how God has always overcome the power of evil through His omnipotence and majesty.

Pay attention to the Word of the Lord and you will see how He always transformed defeat into victory; how He made the weak strong; how He transformed the pitch-black darkness into radiant light.

Put your faith and trust in God and you will step from the darkness of your despair into the glorious light of His love. Equipped by faith you can live in the light.

Lord Jesus, I put all my trust and faith
in You. In Your strength I can
overcome the darkest of times. Amen.

Answer God's Call

At that time men began to call on the name of the LORD.

GENESIS 4:26

There has never been a time in history when people did not have a relationship with God. In our Scripture verse for today, people began to call on the name of God. They called on Him because they needed someone to make sense of the bewildering and unsettling historical journey they had embarked upon.

Everything seemed to be beyond their strength; too overwhelming and drenched in mystery for their simple minds to fathom. By calling on God they found a Source strong enough to give them direction and help. We too can find God – not by searching for Him, but by answering His call. We can do this through the guidance and strength of Jesus Christ.

Holy God, grant me enough faith to be able to answer Your call. Amen.

Let Jesus Guide You

When anxiety was great within me,
Your consolation brought joy to my soul.

PSALM 94:19

How often have you experienced doubt, loneliness and anxiety? When an important decision has to be made do you find it difficult to make the right choice? If so, you are relying on your own limited insight.

Regardless of the circumstances, put your plans, your doubts, your fears and your problems before the Lord's throne of grace and ask Jesus to be your Guide. Be sensitive to the whisperings and stirrings of the Holy Spirit in your life, and face the future with faith and hope. You can rest assured that the living Christ will be by your side, leading and guiding you.

Lord, let Your kindly light guide me. Help me to understand that I should take life one day at a time and seek Your guidance in everything I do. Amen.

Find Your Strength in God

Be strong in the Lord and in His mighty power.

EPHESIANS 6:10

In order to avoid feeling overwhelmed with anxiety and fear, uncertainty and inadequacy, it is essential to cling to Christ and draw your strength from Him. No one else but God knows you and your problems so intimately and completely, God loves you so much that He keeps a vigil of all-embracing love over you.

Armed with the assurance that you are supported and protected by the power, omnipotence, love and mercy of God, you should be equipped to deal with any situation that life might hand you.

Thank You for providing me with armor and shielding me against the shrewdness of Satan. You are my power and my strength. In You, Lord, I trust. Amen.

Productive Faith

He touched their eyes and said, "According
to your faith will it be done to you."

MATTHEW 9:29

There are people who regard faith as a mere
commodity, something that you have a lot or
very little of, depending on the circumstances.

You should, however, understand the importance of maintaining a disposition of expectation towards life. Only those who have an
unfailing faith and trust in the Eternal God can
face the future with courage and serenity. This
great truth, and the acceptance of it in your life
creates stability and enables you to face the future with confidence.

*Help me Lord, to be steadfast in my faith and to be
forever devoted to Your work. Bless me in abundance
and help me to use it to Your greater glory. Amen.*

Allow Faith to Dispel Fear

He said to His disciples, "Why are you so afraid?
Do you still have no faith?"

MARK 4:40

There are few people who do not harbor fear in one form or another. It is a strange fact that many people cannot explain the fear that haunts them but it is nevertheless a burning presence in their lives.

There is only one sure cure for a life that is dominated by fear, and that is a living faith in Jesus Christ. Fear and faith cannot co-exist in the same life. Faith nurtures faith and fear nurtures fear. Place your trust in God.

At first, in the little things in your life, His love and wisdom will be revealed and confirmed, and in time, the bigger things in your life will be under His control too.

As Your child, I know where to find veritable peace.
Dispel fear and selfishness from my heart,
so that I may serve You faithfully. Amen.

Confront Your Weaknesses

David found strength in the LORD his God.

1 SAMUEL 30:6

There are few people who can honestly say that they are equipped to meet and handle any situation with ease and confidence.

Regardless of what problems you face or how inadequate you might feel in any given situation – be it in the business world, on the home front, on the sports field, or even on a social level – you must surrender it in prayer to God. Ask Him to give you strength to handle the situation. Once you accept this and believe that He can and will do it, you can move forward with confidence in the knowledge that God's grace is sufficient to enable you to overcome your weaknesses.

Lord, even when I am filled with doubt; You are by my side. You give me strength to overcome daily temptation, so that one day I may behold Your splendor. Amen.

Walking with God

Noah was a righteous man, blameless among
the people of his time, and he walked with God.

GENESIS 6:9

The quality of your life is largely dependent on the company you keep. The people you associate with can have a far-reaching influence on you – negative as well as positive.

However, there is one influence that can bring only good to your life, and that is the influence of the Holy Spirit when you accept the Lord Jesus Christ as your mentor. Because Jesus is the personification of God's love, it goes without saying that in Him we are able to find everything that is good, praiseworthy, true, honorable, righteous, pure, virtuous and lovely.

Let your life be influenced by the living Christ. Then your life will reflect those qualities that can only come from God.

*Forsaking all else, Lord Jesus, I open my
life to the influence of the Holy Spirit. Amen.*

Steadfast in Faith

"Be strong," declares the LORD, "and work.
For I am with you," declares the LORD Almighty.

HAGGAI 2:4

In the initial exciting phase of a person's born-again life, the Lord's work is done with zeal and enthusiasm. We are filled with the joy of a new life in Christ and we wish to share our feelings and ecstasy with others.

Whatever happens, do not succumb to the temptation to give up your work for Christ. Seek advice, help and guidance at all times but never allow discouragement to paralyze you in your honest pursuit to serve the Lord. Take courage and be steadfast in faith – through the mercy of Jesus Christ you will achieve success.

Your Creation, Lord, will never perish; it is everlasting. Grant me the strength and make me Your servant so that I may share in the fulfillment of Your will. Amen.

march

THE ESSENCE OF LOVE

Tremendous Love

*This is love: not that we loved God, but that He loved us
and sent His Son as an atoning sacrifice for our sins.*

1 JOHN 4:10

Never lose sight of the fact that God loves you. His love is so unfathomable that in the birth, suffering and death of His Son, He assures you of forgiveness and redemption.

Jesus, who was without sin, took our sins upon Himself to redeem and sanctify us. He willingly went to the cross and gave His life in exchange for your deliverance from the yoke of Satan. Such is the magnitude of His grace and love!

If God then was willing to pay such a great price for your salvation, it follows logically that He loves you tremendously. You are very precious to Him and He only wants what is best for you.

*Loving God, thank You for the incredible gift of love
and salvation we have in Jesus Christ. Amen.*

God's Redeeming Love

To them God has chosen to make known among
the Gentiles the glorious riches of this mystery,
which is Christ in you, the hope of glory.

COLOSSIANS 1:27

The wonder of the Christian gospel is that God loved us while we were still sinners. Without such a love we would indeed have still been lost.

As you become deeply aware of your imperfections and sin, you are also aware that there is an all-powerful Deity who is calling you to a better and nobler life. Because of our sinfulness it is impossible to live life as God intended for us without His help.

So accept God's offer to recreate and transform your life. Allow the Holy Spirit to fill you with the strength you need to walk according to God's ways.

Lord, I am sincerely grateful that You bore my punishment for sin and opened the way for me to come to the Father and live according to His ways. Amen.

True Love

Love must be sincere.

ROMANS 12:9

The word *love* is probably the most used and least understood word in any language.

Jesus Christ came to demonstrate the meaning of true love when He willingly gave His life for all humanity. He took our punishment upon Himself to redeem us from our sinfulness. As He said, "Greater love has no one than this, that he lay down his life for his friends" (John 15:13).

True love involves making sacrifices for the sake of another. It is patient and understanding, even in the most trying circumstances. It involves forgiveness and giving of yourself for the benefit of others. It means to love others as Jesus loves you.

Loving Lord Jesus, help me to spread Your love in the world around me. Amen.

True Christianity

Examine yourselves to see whether
you are in the faith; test yourselves. Do
you not realize that Christ Jesus is in you?

2 CORINTHIANS 13:5

Many people have the misconception that Christians are weak, dull, and ineffective; purposefully cutting themselves off from the rest of the world.

There was nothing weak, commonplace, or ineffective about Jesus Christ. The Scriptures bear witness to His humanity and His divinity; to His firmness and tenderness; to His courage and humility; and above all, to His love – even when He was subjected to bitter hatred, barbaric torture and death.

This is the example that our Leader set for all Christians to follow. Allow Him to transform you into a strong and effective witness of the powerful truth of the gospel of Christ.

Thank You heavenly Father, that we are more
than conquerors through Your Son and
through Your Holy Spirit. Amen.

Jesus Understands
Because He Loves You

Jesus wept. Then the Jews said,
"See how He loved him!"

JOHN 11:35-36

Some people see Jesus as someone who is distant; concerned only with matters of universal importance, and not the inconsequential details of our personal lives.

This is not true. He has a loving interest in the world He created, as well as in the people for whom His Son died and was resurrected.

Never lose sight of the fact that Jesus is not only your Master, He is also your friend. Because He lived, suffered and died as a human being, He understands human problems and emotions. He endured suffering, as well as disappointment, sorrow and joy. The Son of God laughed and cried just as we do.

Lord Jesus, in You I have found a Friend who is always loving, faithful, and understanding. Amen.

The Holy Spirit —
Cultivator of Love

*God has poured out His love into our hearts
by the Holy Spirit, whom He has given us.*

ROMANS 5:5

The knowledge that Christ lives in you can inspire your thinking, deepen your insight, give you new confidence, create enthusiasm, and bring purpose and meaning to life.

If you love Christ, the Holy Spirit will begin to make you aware of the needs of others and you will be compelled to do something about them. Your words, your attitude, and your willingness to serve others in the power of the Spirit are the result of God's love in your heart.

God Himself is the source of this love, which Jesus Christ demonstrated to us, and the Holy Spirit cultivates in our hearts.

*Holy Spirit, love Divine, glow within this
heart of mine, kindle every high desire,
perish self in Thy pure fire. Amen.*

Instruments of God's Love

"A new command I give you: Love one another.
As I have loved you, so you must love one another."

JOHN 13:34

The Lord is a God of love who cares for His people, who protects His creation, and who came in the person of Christ Jesus to live amongst us as the Prince of Peace.

Everything concerning Jesus speaks of love, peace and grace – even His terrible death on the cross. His mission was to bring peace into the world and to teach people the real meaning of love.

There is an urgent need today that all people should set aside their petty, personal preferences and follow Jesus' example of love. And we can only do this if we walk intimately with Christ. Then we become instruments of His love and grace.

*Father God, make me an instrument of
Your love. Open my heart to others, so that
I may love them like You love me. Amen.*

God's Great Gift

May the grace of the Lord Jesus Christ,
and the love of God, and the fellowship
of the Holy Spirit be with you all.

2 CORINTHIANS 13:14

When we reflect on the sacrifice God made on Golgotha, through Jesus Christ, for our redemption and salvation, the eternal hope that He gave us through His triumphant resurrection from the dead and the power He extends to us through the Holy Spirit, we are overwhelmed with wonder.

There is no way we could ever repay the Lord for His immeasurable love. But we could, and should, open our lives to Him so that we can pass on His love to others. Christ commanded us to love one another as we love ourselves, and as He loves us.

Lord, I want to glorify You as my Father always.
Guide me, through Your Holy Spirit, so that I will
be obedient to You in everything I do. Amen.

The Extent of God's Love

"I have loved you," says the LORD.
"But you ask, 'How have You loved us?'"

MALACHI 1:2

In the midst of personal setbacks and trage-
dies, in hardships and disappointments, many
people blame God and even turn their backs on
Him because they judge God by human standards.

Tragically they do not see that the disasters
of this world cannot be ascribed to a lack of
love in the Father or the Son, but rather to the
foolishness of man.

The love of God is revealed in His abundant
blessing, His all-powerful forgiveness, His mercy, His promise of eternal life, His comfort, His
gift of the Holy Spirit, and above all, the sacrifice of Jesus Christ on Golgotha. Do we need
more proof than this?

Lord Jesus, I thank You for the privilege of knowing
You. Thank You for taking me out of darkness and
placing me in Your kingdom of light. Amen.

The Power of God's Love

*"You have let go of the commands of God
and are holding on to the traditions of men."*

MARK 7:8

Rituals and traditions play an important role in society. While it is essential that any group of people must adhere to rules so that everything can run smoothly, it is of the utmost importance that these rules do not become the dominant factor in the Christian community.

The foundation of any congregation must be absolute surrender, devotion and obedience to God. Jesus Christ must be central in all things and His will must take precedence over the will of people.

To be a channel of the love of God, surrender yourself unconditionally to the guidance of the Holy Spirit, then you will be able to serve your community according to God's will, and in love.

*Holy Spirit, bring me to total surrender, devotion,
and obedience to the God of love. Amen.*

God's Love Has No Price

Peter answered: "May your money perish
with you, because you thought you could
buy the gift of God with money!"

ACTS 8:20

Many people believe that money can buy them everything. While this may be true of material possessions, it cannot buy things like peace, joy and fullness of life. These qualities have no price tags. They are God's gifts of grace to us.

We enjoy everything that is good and worthwhile by the grace of God. We don't deserve these things, we cannot earn them and we are not worthy of them, but we receive them because of Christ's unfathomable love and grace towards us.

Never take the blessings that you receive from His hand for granted. Always remember that they are gifts of God's eternal goodness and a sign of His love towards you.

I want to thank You for the undeserved gifts
that You bestow so graciously on my life –
for love and peace and hope. Amen.

Incredible but True

Now these three remain: faith, hope and love. But the greatest of these is love.

1 CORINTHIANS 13:13

In these troublesome times, it is hard to remember that love triumphs. Thousands of years ago, Christ was unjustly tried and mocked by the Roman soldiers and cruelly nailed to a wooden cross.

Our awe of Christ on the cross lies in the fact that in the midst of public scorn, derision and unbearable pain, He prayed for those who crucified Him. His love surpassed all the powers of hatred.

When crime and violence make a mockery of all that Jesus Christ lived for and taught, then remember Golgotha and focus on God's love. You will find peace and calm that will make you aware of the immortality and invincibility of love.

God, I ask that love will be the motivating factor of my life, as it is for Yours. Amen.

Surrounded by God's Love

"For them I sanctify Myself, that they
too may be truly sanctified."

JOHN 17:19

There are probably times in your life when your Christian walk seems like a struggle and your faith grows weak. When this happens, shift your focus and look at your life from Christ's viewpoint. His involvement in your life of faith is more important than your own. He is the one who called you.

This divine calling does not depend on your shifting emotions. The Lord will bind you to Him with cords of love. When you become despondent, remember that He will never change. You still belong to Him, He loves you and He is still your Lord. Christ's love for you doesn't change according to your emotions; it is eternal and unfailing.

*I thank You, O Guide, that my changing emotions
need not dictate the course of my life. Thank You
that Your love for me is constant. Amen.*

The Extent of Christ's Love

*Do you show contempt for the riches of His kindness,
tolerance and patience, not realizing that God's
kindness leads you towards repentance?*

ROMANS 2:4

When you consider all the evil in the world, you become aware of the full extent of God's love. People ignore Him, they forget His grace, they disobey Him, they rebel against Him, and they blame Him when things go wrong.

No human being would have tolerated the attitude that mankind displays toward God, and still show the infinite love that God does toward His people. Acknowledge His merciful acceptance of you as His child. Surrender yourself unconditionally to His Son. Praise Him, follow Him and live life to the full as He offers it to you.

God of love, thank You that Your love and grace enabled me to find You. I surrender myself in renewed love to You. Amen.

The Power of God's Love

People will oppress each other – man against man, neighbor against neighbor. The young will rise up against the old, the base against the honorable.

ISAIAH 3:5

In today's world it seems as if chaos and anarchy rule in every corner. However, this doesn't mean we need to tolerate the situation. In Christ Jesus, God came to fight against evil. He did this with the only weapon effective enough to overcome the forces of darkness. And it is just as powerful today – godly love.

God continues to spread His love over His children and it is the Christian's privilege and duty to share this love with others.

There is no other way of stopping the tide of evil that is threatening society today than to try to become a channel of God's love.

Holy God, make me an ambassador of Your love, sharing it with everyone I meet. Amen.

To Abide in Christ's Love

*"As the Father loved Me, I also have
loved you; abide in My love."*

JOHN 15:9 (NKJV)

Jesus loves His disciples, but how often do you
wake up in the morning and thank Him for
that love by telling Him of your sincere love
for Him? What an inspiration it is to wake up
in the morning and to whisper, "Living Lord
Jesus, I love You with all my heart!"

Jesus Christ has promised that if we realize
our dependence upon Him, we will be enabled
to do things which normally would be well
beyond our ability. You can never reach your
full potential until you are united with the living Christ in love. He reminds us that without
Him we can do nothing, but by abiding in His
love our vision is extended and our strength
increased.

*Living and loving Savior, I love You with
all my heart, all my soul and all my strength.
Thank You for Your gracious love for me. Amen.*

Love without Boundaries

They crucified Him. Dividing up His clothes,
they cast lots to see what each would get.

MARK 15:24

Throughout the ages people have rejected, ignored, denied and betrayed Jesus. Yet despite this, in times of need they still call on Him and ask for His help.

The marvel of the Christian faith is that regardless of how you treat Christ, He still loves you. He lavishes His boundless love on you and meets your needs.

The crucifixion shows us that the love of Christ knows no boundaries. It is a love so sincere and pure that nothing can withstand it. Whether you deserve it or not – this is the love that God wants to give to you through Jesus Christ. How then can you withhold your love from Him?

Lord, I want to share in the glory of Your love.
Fill me with Your love so that I can truly
love You as You deserve. Amen.

Love Brings Life

We know that we have passed from death to life,
because we love our brothers.

1 JOHN 3:14

Everything Jesus was, everything He taught, and everything He did, was a manifestation of God's love. The love of God enriches the lives of everyone who allows Him to pour it into their hearts.

It is possible to experience the love of God firsthand and to allow your life to become a channel of God's love. This is the wisest way we can choose to live. The opposite of love is hate. Hate follows the path of bitterness, dissension and torn apart relationships.

When the love of God is a powerful force in your life and His love reaches out to others through you, your own life is enriched in a way you never thought possible.

Lord God, through Your Holy Spirit please do
the impossible and enrich my life through
the wonders of Your love. Amen.

Receive God's Love

He predestined us to be adopted as His sons through
Jesus Christ, in accordance with His pleasure and will.

EPHESIANS 1:5

If the name and character of Jesus had not been love, it would have been impossible for imperfect and sinful people to enter into a relationship with Him. But because He is love, He calls you to Him.

As you open up your life to His influence, the Holy Spirit will enable you to live as God intended: in His strength and in the awareness of His living presence.

When God's love fills your life, you will experience a feeling of unity with Him. This intimacy isn't something that you can earn through your own efforts; it is a gift from God. It becomes yours when you receive it in faith and with gratitude.

Eternal God, Your unfathomable love is beyond
my understanding, yet You have given it to
me as a precious gift of Your grace. Amen.

God's Unfailing Love

"Though the mountains be shaken and the hills be removed, yet My unfailing love for you will not be shaken nor My covenant of peace be removed."

ISAIAH 54:10

Most of us have experienced firsthand how the radically changing circumstances of life often have a dramatic influence on us, and on those whom we love. One moment we experience joy, the next we are swept into the depths of despair.

Regardless of these unexpected and unplanned events in your life, you have the assurance of God's love for you. However despondent you may be, never lose sight of the fact that Jesus loves you with an unfailing, eternal and perfect love.

Turn to Him in times of affliction and you will enjoy the blessings of the Lord, as well as His love that drives out all fear.

Lord, I feel safe in the palm of Your hand.
Thank You for sheltering me when the
storms of life rage around me. Amen.

God Loves You

We know that in all things God works for the
good of those who love Him, who have
been called according to His purpose.

ROMANS 8:28

People often cannot understand why trials and
setbacks happen to them. Yet one of the basic
components of Christianity is steadfast faith
in the love of God. This love has been proven
beyond a doubt in the gift of His Son to a lost
world. That is why in every situation of life,
you can put your trust in the wisdom and
goodness of a loving Father.

When you find yourself facing problems or
setbacks, remember that your life is in God's
mighty hands. Because of His great love for you,
everything that happens to you has a purpose.

*Jesus, in the darkest moments of my life, thank You
that I can be assured of the goodness of Your love
that lets nothing happen to me by chance. Amen.*

Let Your Love Be Selfless

*Let us not love with words or
tongue but with actions and in truth.*

1 JOHN 3:18

True love is not easily fathomed. Yet, of all the human emotions it is the most profound. We tend to reduce love to mushy sentimentality, thus diminishing it as a dynamic force and making it powerless and ineffective.

The basis for true love is identification with the loved one. It is to experience his or her joys, sorrows, temptations and disappointments. True love involves sacrifice and sorrow. The true quality of love surpasses sympathy and sentimentality, and manifests itself in loyalty and faithfulness.

Love in action is more than simply doing good deeds, pure love is profound and unselfish and embraces the faithfulness and noble principles that enrich the heart and mind of a person. It is precious above all things.

*Father, enable me to love without
counting the cost. Amen.*

Love Is Practical
and Sincere

This is how God showed His love among us:
He sent His one and only Son into the
world that we might live through Him.

1 JOHN 4:9

Jesus Christ was deeply practical. If you study His life you will note that, along with the profound spirituality of His ministry, He had a truly practical nature. When Jesus raised Jairus's daughter from the dead, He told her parents to give her something to eat.

True love and care requires more than mere words – it calls for action. It is to support someone in prayer, but also to do something practical to show your love; even if it is inconvenient.

By demonstrating your love for others in a practical way, you follow the example Jesus set for us. He is our example because His love exceeds all other love.

Holy Jesus, help me to love others with a love
that is practical and sincere. Amen.

Love Is the
Most Excellent Way

Now I will show you the most excellent way.

1 CORINTHIANS 12:31

Jesus was the embodiment of God's perfect love. He calls us to walk the path of this love. No compromise can be tolerated. If we wish to follow the most excellent way, we must follow the way of His love.

A response to the challenge of Christian love calls for deep devotion. Even when you have given everything, you still want to give more. It is then that you open your life to the influence of the Holy Spirit. That which you cannot achieve by your own effort and strength, God will achieve through you.

His Holy Spirit residing in us makes the impossible possible. Choose the best – choose to love!

Lord, reveal Your love in my life so that I may
love my neighbor. Help me to aspire to
this commandment of Yours. Amen.

True Love Allows Freedom

He came to that which was His own,
but His own did not receive Him.

JOHN 1:11

If you love someone you allow him or her the freedom that their spirit needs. It is only by setting someone free that the bonds of mutual love may be strengthened.

The principle of generous love forms the basis of the Christian gospel. God allows you the freedom of choice to either believe in Him or reject Him. Christ does not want to compel you to love Him. He invited you by grace to accept Him and to associate with Him through a new relationship of love.

If you accept His love and make His way of life your own, you will delightfully discover that your imperfect love reacts to His divine love. Such a love brings about freedom, joy and peace in your life.

Take away my weariness, Lord, and allow Your
strength to flow through me. Amen.

Establish Healthy Relationships

Be kind and compassionate to one another, forgiving each other, just as in Christ God forgave you.

EPHESIANS 4:32

In life it is important to protect yourself against selfishness, foolish pride, unkind thoughts and other negative traits.

If you harden yourself against calls for help or pleas for forgiveness, you harden your spirit.

The way to overcome an indifferent attitude is to approach life with the attitude of Jesus Christ. Do not condemn, instead have understanding and sympathy toward others.

A compassionate attitude allows the Spirit of God to work through you and bring you to the realization that only by being a blessing to your fellow man can you receive the love and blessing of God.

Sometimes we are so indifferent to the world around us. Help us, Lord, to support others in neighborly love. Amen.

The Christian's Deepest Desire

I want to know Christ.

PHILIPPIANS 3:10

To be a Christian means knowing Christ and loving Him dearly. Jesus often taught that it is difficult to live isolated from love.

Love, because of its intrinsic nature, rises above all differences of race, color and denomination. Because love is the determining factor in life, it cannot be confined to the limitations of the human mind and experience. It must flow from the Christian in order to be seen, to inspire, to heal and to encourage. Our desire must be to know Christ better and to serve Him better in love.

Such a love cannot be created by human emotion and desire because God is its origin and source.

Lord, teach me to be strong and faithful in my love for You and also to love my neighbor as myself. Amen.

Bound to Christ

Who shall separate us from the love of Christ?

ROMANS 8:35

Paul asks a penetrating question here. He implies that nothing can separate us from the love of Christ. He even mentions things that could attempt to do so: trouble or hardship, persecution, famine or nakedness, danger or sword. He comes to the conclusion that nothing will be able to separate us "from the love of God that is in Christ Jesus our Lord" (Rom. 8:39).

The Father loves you. This truth should give you comfort, strength and encouragement. Although it is a fact that God's love surrounds you, many people do not experience it because they erect barriers against it. Break down those barriers so that you may experience God's love in your life daily.

Holy Spirit, make me aware of You residing in me, so that my life will reflect Your glory and love. Amen.

The Song of Love

*If I speak in the tongues of men and of angels,
but have not love, I am only a resounding
gong or a clanging cymbal.*

1 CORINTHIANS 13:1

This chapter unlocks all the noble qualities of love. Here, Paul speaks about the path of love. He begins by saying that one can possess any spiritual gift, but if it does not bear the stamp of love, it is useless.

If love is not an integral part of miracles, of sacrifice, or of our spoken and intellectual gifts, then they are fruitless. The gift of intellectual excellence without love leads to intellectual snobbery. Knowledge lit by the fire of love is the only kind of knowledge that can save people. None of these are worth anything if they do not go hand-in-hand with true love.

*Lord, my God, I thank You that all the love in my life
is but a mere stepping stone towards You. Amen.*

Love Forgets about Self

Love does not boast.

1 CORINTHIANS 13:4

Boasting is a negative form of love also known as self-love. True love is selfless. It would rather confess unworthiness than boast of its own achievements. Some people give their love as though they were bestowing an honor on the receiver. That is not love; that is conceit.

The one that truly loves cannot stop marveling at the fact that there is someone who loves him. Love is kept humble in the knowledge that it could never make a sufficiently worthy sacrifice for the one it loves.

This also applies to our spiritual lives. We dare not accept God's love as a matter of course as if we deserved it. Such pride robs us of the blessing and spiritual growth that God has in mind for us.

Lord, keep me humble in my love, so that it does not become the cause of pride and arrogance. Amen.

Love Keeps No Record of Wrongs

Love keeps no record of wrongs.

1 CORINTHIANS 13:5

Godly love does not hold on to every bad memory of people who have sinned against it. Yet often, people do not want to forget their hatred and revengeful thoughts. They become collectors of grievances and this process poisons their souls and drives the love from their hearts.

Many people fuel their anger in order to keep it alive. They brood on the mistakes made against them until it becomes impossible for them to forget.

Christian love teaches the great lesson of forgiving and forgetting. If you keep a record of the wrongs committed against you, you are inclined to miss the noble, good and beautiful things in life.

Holy Spirit, grant me the heavenly gift of forgiving and forgetting. Amen.

april

PRAYING POWER

The Holy Spirit and Prayer

*Live by the Spirit, and you will not gratify
the desires of the sinful nature.*

GALATIANS 5:16

Many of us desire to have a meaningful prayer life; to set aside more time for God and grow in our relationship with Him, but time and again we fail.

To triumph over Satan's attempts to distract us in our prayer time is not easy. Yet Jesus promised the help of the Holy Spirit to those who embrace Him as their Lord and Savior. "The Spirit helps us in our weakness" (Rom. 8:26).

Open yourself up to the influence of the Holy Spirit, be obedient to His guidance, and you will find that your prayer life will change dramatically – for the better.

*Lord Jesus, let me always pray, give testimony,
and serve with love. Teach me to act in response
to the guidance of Your Spirit. Amen.*

Prayer: The Challenge

Being in anguish, He prayed more earnestly.

LUKE 22:44

There are enriching moments in prayer when you experience glorious intimacy with God and are filled with inexpressible joy. But true prayer often has a seriousness that touches on the deeper issues of life.

When you pray that God will help you grow spiritually, or show you the right way to live, or use you in His service, you will experience the full impact of the challenge of prayer.

Such prayers are essentially between you and God, but you will soon discover that they touch other people as well. As God lays people on your heart, you begin to understand the responsibility of prayer. Sharing in this privilege strengthens you to live in love towards God and your fellow man.

Lord, I pray that my heart would be overwhelmed
by the love of God so that I can truly love
and pray for those around me. Amen.

Pray for Discernment

Your righteousness is everlasting and Your law is true.
Trouble and distress have come upon me,
but Your commands are my delight.

PSALM 119:142–143

The trials and tribulations of life often force us to turn to someone or something for help. The psalmist, however, knew it was best to turn to God for wisdom and discernment.

He asked of God, "Give me understanding that I may live." He knew that God's plan for his life would preserve him from wrongful actions and would destroy the path of the foolish. Therefore he chose to delight himself in God and to uphold His statutes.

God promises to grant us wisdom if we ask Him for it (see James 1:5).

Pray to God for discernment and wisdom in your struggle and ask Him to teach you what you need to know so you can apply His wisdom to your situation.

*Heavenly Father, I am Your redeemed servant and
I ask for wisdom and discernment. Amen.*

An Effective Prayer Life

Do not be anxious about anything, but in everything,
by prayer and petition, with thanksgiving,
present your requests to God.

PHILIPPIANS 4:6

Of all the Christian disciplines, prayer is the most commonly practiced and the least understood. Prayer should not be regarded as a life jacket in desperate times or as a wish list.

We begin by establishing a relationship of prayer with God. Develop an understanding of the living Christ, study His Word and meditate on His presence.

Thank and praise God for the privilege of prayer, and then cast all your cares, fears, problems and requests on Him and ask Him to grant you what He knows you need, as well as the grace to handle any situation that might arise. If you do this, God's plan will soon begin to unfold in your life.

You grant us more than we could ever ask for. We
always have the blessed assurance of Your love
and know that Your promises hold good. Amen.

Prayer Is the Key

My purpose is … that they may have the full riches of complete understanding, in order that they may know the mystery of God, namely, Christ, in whom are hidden all the treasures of wisdom and knowledge.

COLOSSIANS 2:2-3

Many Christians are ignorant of God's boundless grace. Their need blinds them to the One who could supply their needs if they would only trust Him.

Time and again Scripture reiterates that the Father is more willing to give than we are to receive. We are constantly reminded that if we pray and believe, we will receive that which we pray for. Prayer is the key that unlocks the treasure chambers of God.

How God is going to answer your prayers is neither your responsibility nor your concern. A simple childlike faith that looks to God and believes unconditionally that He answers prayer is the kind of prayer that God answers with joy.

Lord, thank You for the key of prayer with which we can unlock Your precious blessings. Amen.

What Is the Focus of Your Prayers?

"Since you have asked for this and not for long life or wealth for yourself ... but for discernment in administering justice, I will do what you have asked."

1 KINGS 3:11–12

There is a strong temptation to focus on "self" in prayer. Many people only come before God with lists of requests. The danger is that your prayers become self-centered and your gratitude to God and to others take a back seat.

Every prayer that you pray must echo the immortal words of Christ, "Not as I will, but as You will" (Matt. 26:39). This is the highest practice in faith – complete surrender to God's will and committing yourself to Him. In this way you acknowledge His sovereignty over your life and your circumstances.

Christ has His hand on you, and the Holy Spirit will guide you onto the perfect path.

Lord, You guide me when words fail me in prayer. Your mercy intervenes and gives me peace. Amen.

Surrender Your Life to God

Lord, teach us to pray.

LUKE 11:1

Most Christians are very aware of their inability to pray according to the will of God. Christ sacrificed Himself for us. He gave Himself freely, but He will enrich your life only as far as you allow Him to.

The depth and quality of your devotion to Him will be reflected in the strength of your prayer life. It does not mean a thing to ask God for a meaningful and positive prayer life unless you do your share to develop it.

If you surrender yourself more completely to Christ, you will become increasingly aware of His living presence in your prayer life.

Lord, teach me not to fret about what tomorrow may bring. Teach me to quietly trust in You, because You are good and all-wise. Amen.

Be Fervent and Persevere in Prayer

So He left them and went away once more and prayed the third time, saying the same thing.

MATTHEW 26:44

Some Christians wonder why, if the Father is all-seeing and omniscient, they still need to persevere in the discipline of prayer. They feel guilty about troubling God over and over with issues that He is already aware of.

Remember, you often know about problems in other people's lives, but you do not usually intervene unless asked to do so. If you feel that a particular matter in your life needs God's intervention, do not hesitate to bring it before Him. Remind Him of His promises and ask Him to take care of the situation.

God will never tire of listening to you if you come to Him in the name of Christ.

In distress I call to You, O Lord, because only You can grant me peace. Thank You for hearing my prayers and for always answering my cry for help. Amen.

Take Time to Pray

None of us lives to himself alone.

ROMANS 14:7

People always find the time to do the things they want to do, but are quick to find excuses for not doing the things they don't want to do. This happens in our spiritual lives, too.

If you are making excuses as to why you can't pray or spend time with God, ask yourself why you are making these excuses. Why is your prayer life without power? Why has your faith become a burden instead of an inspiration of hope and faith?

This happens when you no longer reach out to God in prayer, or if you only ever express your personal desires. True prayer broadens your spiritual and intellectual horizons, and makes your relationship with the Savior more profound.

O Lord, please help me to develop a meaningful
and powerful prayer life under the guidance
of the Holy Spirit. Amen.

A Life Carried by Prayer

Therefore do not be unwise, but
understand what the will of the Lord is.

EPHESIANS 5:17 (NKJV)

Prayer is always of cardinal importance in every matter. It is your communication with God and therefore also the foundation of your Christian lifestyle. Because this is the case, every action in your life should be supported and carried by prayer.

If you spend quality time in the presence of the Master and you open up your heart and mind to Him, He will speak to you through His Holy Spirit. This may be through circumstances which occur, or you may know instinctively what to do. Whatever the case may be, if you are sensitively tuned in to the voice of the Holy Spirit, God's will, will be revealed to you. Therefore in everything you do, turn to God in prayer. Only then can you live according to His will.

O Holy Spirit, make me aware of God's voice in my
life. Let me hear Him clearly above the hum drum
of the world so that I may do His will. Amen.

Pray – Regardless …

*When my life was ebbing away, I remembered You, Lord,
and my prayer rose to You, to Your holy temple.*

JONAH 2:7

Many people deny themselves the privilege of
the peace of God, simply because they feel too
undeserving to talk to God.

Yet Jesus promised that He will not cast out
anybody who comes to Him. He also says that
He did not come to call the righteous, but sinners, to salvation. Throughout the Scriptures
you can read of His mercy and love that reach
out to all people: the good and the bad, the
worthy and the unworthy.

However unworthy you may feel at this
moment, reach out to Him in prayer and He
will take you by the hand – and nobody will
snatch you from Him.

*Father, I want to live my life glorifying You. Help me
not to lose sight of You when times are difficult. Guide
me towards obedience through Your Spirit. Amen.*

Pray without Pause

Pray continually.

1 THESSALONIANS 5:17

It is difficult to create a pattern of prayer in your life. It is even more difficult to cultivate a sustained prayer life.

The motive behind sustained prayer is to listen to God and to be sensitive to His guidance through the Holy Spirit. In the quiet of your deepest being you will feel His presence and experience His omnipotence. Regardless of where you may find yourself, or what you may busy yourself with, you can lift your heart to God, even for a single moment and in a fleeting thought, and in doing so, experience the reality of His presence.

Thank You, Lord, for hearing my prayers of supplication and thanksgiving, and that You bless those who wait on You in prayer. Help me to maintain a childlike trust in You – now and forever. Amen.

Prayer Is a Spiritual Discipline

After He had dismissed them, He went up
on a mountainside by Himself to pray.
When evening came, He was there alone.

MATTHEW 14:23

Everyone who yearns to develop a meaningful spiritual life must be willing to be disciplined. Without discipline faith has emotion, but lacks the quality for spiritual growth.

The most important component in the development of a stable and positive faith is the nurturing of a living and powerful prayer life. The Master, our Example in prayer, kept a conscientious watch over His times of personal prayer, even dismissing His most intimate friends to be alone with God. This means that your devotional appointments with God should be kept faithfully and conscientiously.

I call out to You, O Lord, and cast my sorrows,
my doubts and my needs on You, because I know
that You will hear my prayer. Amen.

Prayer Is Essential

Very early in the morning, while it was still dark,
Jesus got up, left the house and went off to a
solitary place, where He prayed.

MARK 1:35

Some of God's children are just too busy. Even if you are extremely busy in the service of the Lord but are not supported by the power of faithful prayer while you work, you run the risk of a complete breakdown and burnout of your spiritual life. You cannot fulfill your spiritual duty without prayer.

Prayer is the encouragement and inspiration for Christian service. It gives sincerity to everything that you embark on in the Master's name and gives you a deep satisfaction that you cannot get from any other source.

Father, through Your favor, may I experience more comfort in times of adversity, more sorrow over sin, more joy in my labors. May I be inspired by prayer and pursue Your example diligently. Amen.

Make Prayer Your Motivational Power

"When you pray, do not keep on babbling like pagans, for they think they will be heard because of their many words."

MATTHEW 6:7

There are many people who do not give serious thought to their prayers to God. They have a fixed pattern that used to be meaningful but through repetition has lost its meaning.

When you spend time in the presence of the living God, and you are sharing your wishes with Him, you must be seriously mindful of the guidance of the Holy Spirit. Ask Him while you pray if there is anything that you can do to make your prayer life more fertile. Believe in your prayers and then leave everything in God's hands and see how He works in your life.

Father, through Christ I wish to glorify You as my Father. Grant that I, through the guidance of Your Holy Spirit, may be obedient in my quiet times with You. Amen.

A Devotional Exercise

Be joyful in hope, patient in affliction, faithful in prayer.

ROMANS 12:12

Do you get the maximum spiritual satisfaction from your devotional time? How you answer this question reveals the difference between an ineffective prayer life, and one filled with an awareness of the presence of God.

In your everyday life, the opportunities for prayer become incalculable. Send up brief prayers for those who seem to be tired or disillusioned or pray thoughts of joy with those who are joyful. You need never be at a loss for things to pray for, provided you practice prayer in every situation of life.

By broadening your devotional base, your devotional times with God become more profound. While practicing praying for others, you are strengthening your ties with Jesus Christ.

Lord God, thank You that I may come to You in prayer for advice and guidance. Thank You for Your Spirit that teaches us to pray. Amen.

Be Patient in Prayer

I will stand at my watch and station myself on the ramparts; I will look to see what He will say to me, and what answer I am to give to this complaint.

HABAKKUK 2:1

So often people complain that their prayers remain unheard. They become impatient with God and their faith weakens.

Yet it is an established and irrefutable fact that God hears and answers our prayers. However, we need to know His Word to understand that His answer comes in His perfect time, and in His perfect way, according to His perfect will. This is also done according to our needs – not our wishes and will, unless they are in accordance with God.

Truly effective prayer often requires us to watch and wait. He will reveal Himself to us and show us His way in His good time.

Father, grant that in times of doubt I will turn to You, that I will hold on to Your constancy and on to the assurance that I have in Jesus Christ. Amen.

Peace in Prayer

Devote yourselves to prayer,
being watchful and thankful.

COLOSSIANS 4:2

There are many people whose lives are ruined by anxiety, worry and fear. Paul says, "Do not be anxious about anything, but in everything, by prayer and petition, with thanksgiving, present your requests to God. And the peace of God, which transcends all understanding, will guard your hearts and your minds in Christ Jesus" (Phil. 4:6-7).

Especially in times of adversity, there is absolutely nothing that you can do in your own strength to solve your problem. Jesus said that without Him we can do nothing, but take heart because He also said that in God, all thing are possible.

How wonderful, Lord, that I may come to You
when I am sad and when I repent of my sins.
Thank You for hearing my prayers. Amen.

Wisdom Comes through Prayer

Praise be to the name of God for ever and ever;
wisdom and power are His. He gives wisdom
to the wise and knowledge to the discerning.

DANIEL 2:20–21

Prayer holds many great advantages for those who make it part of their daily routine. To wait patiently in the presence of God creates an opportunity to experience the Holy Spirit. It can transform a time of senseless words into a source of strength and wisdom that restores balance to your life.

God talks to you through prayer. Whether you are plagued by doubt or confusion, or whether you are finding it difficult to make a decision, the person who prays will be enlightened and guided. Prayer confirms the existence of God in your heart and brings with it a new experience of life and wisdom.

*Jesus, Savior, Your burden is light and
Your yoke is easy. Help me to take up
my cross daily and follow You. Amen.*

Miracles through Prayer

Praise be to the LORD, for He has heard my cry
for mercy. The LORD is my strength and my
shield; my heart trusts in Him, and I am helped.

PSALM 28:6-7

Despite the cynicism of our age, God can still perform miracles. Every time someone is healed in answer to prayer, God has performed a miracle. Every time we experience peace in our hearts after a time of tension and suffering, or when our grief finally becomes bearable – then a miracle has occurred.

Hand your problems over to God in prayer today and wait on Him in faith. If there is something you need to do, do it without delay. Do not let despair overwhelm you. In the right time and in the right way, God will answer your prayers and you will be astounded by the results.

*My God and Father, I know that You are powerful
and that You can do far more than I can pray for or
think of because You are the Almighty. Amen.*

Have Faith in Prayer

You do not have, because you do not ask God.
When you ask, you do not receive,
because you ask with wrong motives.

JAMES 4:2–3

One of the most common complaints is, "God doesn't answer my prayers." Some people think it is because God is punishing them or because prayer is futile. To them prayer has become a mere formality.

True prayer is to personally experience the presence of the living Christ in your quiet times and throughout the day. It is the joyous assurance that the Lord keeps His promises and that He lives in you and you in Him.

Such prayer becomes a faith exercise that teaches you that, as you lay your requests before the Lord, He will give you what you need according to His wisdom, and you will recognize and accept His answers.

Lord my God, it is with gratitude and
humility that I accept Your will for my life,
for in You is perfect wisdom. Amen.

The Prayer of Jesus

After Jesus said this, He looked toward
heaven and prayed: "Father, the time has come.
Glorify Your Son, that Your Son may glorify You."

JOHN 17:1-2

In preparation for the suffering that Jesus knew He would have to endure in the days ahead, He prayed for God to be glorified in His body at the Last Supper.

How could a terrible death on the cross bring glory to God? Jesus explains in His prayer that God is glorified through the obedience of the Son. We seldom feel that our suffering and defeat could be to God's glory, yet we seldom look at things from a godly perspective.

God's glory is reflected in our deeds of love, obedience and loyalty. Follow Jesus' example today by praying that God will be glorified in your life and by your obedience.

*Loving Father, help me to contribute to
the glory of Your name by doing everything
in obedience to Your will. Amen.*

May You Be Equipped

*May the God of peace ... that great Shepherd of the sheep,
equip you with everything good for doing His will,
and may He work in us what is pleasing to Him.*

HEBREWS 13:20-21

The Bible often refers to the children of God as sheep that are totally dependent on the Shepherd for food and protection. Although we live in a society where individual performance is highly regarded, we should never think that we can be everything that Christ expects from us in our own strength.

We have been brought into a covenant with our Lord and with one another through the sacrificial blood of Christ. Pray that God will equip you, as well as the believers in your community and local congregation, to join forces in doing God's work.

*Lord Jesus, our Good Shepherd,
equip Your children so that they will
want to do Your work together. Amen.*

Prayer for Discernment

Trouble and distress have come upon me,
but Your commands are my delight. Your statutes are
forever right; give me understanding that I may live.

PSALM 119:143–144

The trials and tribulations of life often force us to seek help. We tend to look for a sympathetic ear first but it is always best to turn to God for wisdom.

The psalmist knew that God's plan for him would preserve him from wrongful actions and would destroy the way of the foolish. Therefore, he delighted in God and committed himself to upholding His statutes.

Perhaps you are also struggling with something. God promises to grant us wisdom if we ask Him for it. Pray for discernment in your struggles and ask Him to teach you so that you may apply His wisdom to your situation.

*Heavenly Father, I am Your redeemed servant
and I plead for wisdom and discernment
in everything I do. Amen.*

Prayer for an
Important Decision

So they proposed two men. Then they prayed, "Lord,
You know everyone's heart. Show us which of these two
You have chosen to take over this apostolic ministry."

ACTS 1:23-25

Important decisions cause most of us concern.
We spend hours brooding over the advantages
and disadvantages, when we should actually
just ask God.

The disciples faced an important decision.
As a group they nominated two people who
were sincere followers of Jesus, but they realized that they did not know the hearts of the
two candidates – only God did. Therefore they
entrusted the final choice to God in prayer.

Whenever you need to make a decision, dis-
cuss it with God in prayer. Ask for His wisdom
and guidance; ask Him to reveal His will to you.

Omniscient God, Help me to make decisions in
accordance with Your will. Amen.

Come, Let Us Pray

There on the beach we knelt to pray.

ACTS 21:5

There are people who believe that prayer should be limited to the church or to the privacy of an inner room. They regard public prayer with uneasiness and even disapproval.

Yet prayer is as much a form of communication as a conversation is. Except prayer is a conversation between our heavenly Father and us. There is nothing more natural than this.

While you should never be too shy to pray, it is also necessary to be discreet in terms of the time and place you choose to pray.

Trust in the guidance of the Holy Spirit and your prayers will always be a blessing to you as well as to others.

O Hearer of prayers, thank You that I can draw near to Your sacred throne at all times and under all circumstances, and I know that You will always listen. Amen.

The Path of Prayer

"When you pray, don't babble on and on. Your Father knows exactly what you need even before you ask Him!"

MATTHEW 6:7–8 (NLT)

Repetitive prayers may be a good way to develop the spirit of prayer, but the Lord makes it abundantly clear that prayer becomes ineffective when it deteriorates into the mere recital of pretty phrases.

True prayer is more than words. It is an attitude of the spirit and mind that reaches out to God. Prayer is a two-way process. You tell God what you want from Him and He reveals to you what He expects from you. Prayer is not a series of empty words, but rather an increasingly intimate relationship with the heavenly Father and a sincere desire to do His will.

God and Father, grant me the true spirit of prayer so that my communion with You will become more and more profound and meaningful. Amen.

The Gracious Gift of Prayer

Pray in the Spirit on all occasions with all kinds
of prayers and requests. With this in mind,
be alert and always keep on praying.

EPHESIANS 6:18

What value do you place on prayer? Do you
regard it as a wonderful gift of grace from God,
or as an unbearable burden?

The privilege of prayer is a special gift from
God to us. It is God's personal invitation to you
to enter into His sanctuary, to talk to Him and
listen when He has something to say to you.

Prayer is a discipline that requires preparation and practice. Make time to come quietly
into the presence of God. Focus your attention
on Jesus. Listen and speak to God and thank
Him for the gracious gift of His love for you.
That will enable you to live in an atmosphere
of peace and trust.

*Lord, thank You for the privilege of being able to bring
every aspect of my life to You in prayer. Amen.*

Prayer Is Boundless

At Gibeon the LORD appeared to Solomon
during the night in a dream, and God said,
"Ask for whatever you want Me to give you."

1 KINGS 3:5

Many people get irritated with long-winded people who obscure the real issue behind a flood of words instead of asking something outright.

A similar situation can arise in your prayer life. The Old Testament prayer warriors were completely open and honest when they spoke with the Lord. Their confessions were complete and revealing, their requests were real and humble.

When presenting your requests to the Lord, be specific and honest. Ask for the gifts of wisdom and discernment so that you can recognize and accept His answers.

I want to be completely open when I speak
to You about the situations I am facing today.
I need Your wisdom and discernment.
Please help me to do what is right. Amen.

Prepare Yourself for Life through Prayer

May my prayer be set before You like incense; may the lifting up of my hands be like the evening sacrifice.

PSALM 141:2

The future is unknown but you can prepare for it by developing a healthy prayer life. This will provide you with strength in moments of weakness, and comfort in times of sorrow.

Many people will tell you that praying is a natural instinct. This may be true, but an effective prayer life is the result of a disciplined and sensitive attitude before God.

Share your joy with God in prayer while the sun shines and there will be no anxiety when the storm comes. You will merely share in the quiet conviction that God is in full control and that you have prepared adequately for every situation in life through prayer. God will do the rest!

How wonderful, heavenly Father, to praise and glorify You. I want to sing the praises of Your great love and faithfulness for all nations to hear. Amen.

may

Growing in Christ

Only Jesus

When they looked up, they saw no one except Jesus.

MATTHEW 17:8

Perhaps it is time to pause for a while and examine your spiritual journey under the guidance and leadership of the Holy Spirit. Put all preconceived ideas aside and open up your spirit to His guidance.

It is the all-important sovereignty of Jesus Christ that generates a living faith in your heart. Faith is powerless and meaningless unless it is grounded in Christ and if He rules as King in your life.

If you allow the Holy Spirit to work freely in your life, He will lead you into a deeper and more intimate relationship with Christ. Jesus will begin to occupy the central position in your life.

Desire of my heart, I thank You that my heart thirsts
for You all the time. Protect me from anyone
or anything that could draw me away from
experiencing Your presence in my life. Amen.

Grow in Christ

He is the image of the invisible God.

COLOSSIANS 1:15

Paul says that Jesus Christ and the eternal God are equal – that the One is like the Other.

This truth stirs one's soul, and you may feel that such spiritual heights are beyond your reach. Jesus lived on such a high moral level, setting examples of how to respond in certain situations, that you cannot live up to His example on your own. Yet this truth can also inspire and elevate us.

The living Christ does not condemn people for their sins, but inspires them to reach unprecedented heights. Depending on the strength and intensity of our devotion to Him, we can, in a small way, become like Jesus. And that is God's purpose for your life.

Stand by me, Lord Jesus, help me to grow into the likeness of Your image through the power and guidance of the Holy Spirit. Amen.

Ensure Your Spiritual Growth

Make every effort to be found spotless,
blameless and at peace with Him.

2 PETER 3:14

The point of departure for our spiritual lives is unconditional surrender to the love of Christ. However, afterwards it is essential that we grow. A life starving for spiritual food will never develop to its full potential.

You should care for your spiritual life by nourishing it with the Word of God. In addition you should be aware of the presence of the living Christ. This must happen every day so that He can accompany and guide your growth. His Holy Spirit must reveal to you the true meaning of His eternal Word.

Pay serious attention to it and you will be surprised to discover that you are developing your full spiritual potential.

Master, help me through Your good Spirit to
nourish my spiritual life so that I will grow
to reveal Your nature in my life. Amen.

Cultivating Spiritual Growth

Instead, speaking the truth in love, we will in all things grow up into Him who is the Head, that is, Christ.

EPHESIANS 4:15

Christianity without spiritual growth cannot bring a deep, true joy and satisfaction. When you received Christ into your life, you did not only accept a system of doctrines; you promised eternal faithfulness to Him because you believe in Him. You can only understand Him better if you share your life with Him, and stop focusing on yourself.

Growing in Christ is not an exercise meant to create a comfortable religious feeling far removed from the hard realities of life – it should rather inspire the believer to positive action.

Renew your prayer life; rediscover the Spirit of Christ in the Scriptures and see how growth in Christ will lead you to new dimensions of life.

Lord Jesus, make my faith a dynamic power through the renewal of my prayer life and Bible study. Amen.

Live for Christ

His divine power has given us everything we need
for life and godliness through our knowledge of
Him who called us by His own glory and goodness.

2 PETER 1:3

The call to live a Christian life rings out once again, but some of us are so overwhelmed by the intensity of the task that our faith falters because of our human weakness.

Yet we do not have to rely on our own abilities to serve God at all. Remember that Christ will not call you to any form of service without equipping you for it. He has set the example and all that He expects from you is to follow Him.

If you commit yourself to Him and place your trust in Him completely, He will provide you with everything that you need to truly live.

Heavenly Father, I dedicate myself to Your service anew, in the certain knowledge that You will provide everything that I need to live an abundant life. Amen.

Reach for Spiritual Maturity

When I was a child, I talked like a child,
I thought like a child, I reasoned like a child.
When I became a man, I put childish ways behind me.

1 CORINTHIANS 13:11

Some people's spiritual journey can be compared to a rocking horse: there is a lot of movement, but little progress. They never achieve spiritual maturity because they allow grudges to poison them with bitterness. Allowing a grudge to fester could harm your spirit and hinder your spiritual development.

Today you have an opportunity to grow by God's grace, to put the negative behind you, and to reach for a future of exuberant spiritual growth. If you open your heart to the Holy Spirit's influence, He will help you to forgive and forget – allowing you to concentrate on the things that will bring you spiritual maturity.

Lord, I cannot do anything without You.
Fill me with Your Spirit so that I can grow
and experience fulfillment in You. Amen.

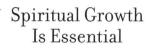

Spiritual Growth Is Essential

I gave you milk, not solid food, for you were not yet ready for it. For since there is jealousy and quarreling among you, are you not worldly?

1 CORINTHIANS 3:2–3

Many people believe that God is great and awesome. In faith they accept that He is love, but refuse to allow Him to fill their lives with that same love. He promised His power to all who serve Him, but they remain weak and powerless. They say they believe in Him, but they don't experience His loving presence.

The Christian way of life is meant to enrich the life of disciples. When you start becoming spiritually mature, you develop a greater love for others. When the love of Christ saturates you, negative attitudes such as pettiness, jealousy and strife are dissolved. And then you can rise above this immaturity and enjoy the solid food that the Holy Spirit gives.

Lord, I want to know more of Your love daily so that I can love others in turn. Amen.

To Live for Christ

For to me, to live is Christ.

PHILIPPIANS 1:21

Too many people live purposeless lives, passing through life with superficial goals. But this type of life cannot bring real satisfaction. Real joy and fulfillment come from having a goal in life that pleases Christ.

Your goal should be to live your life in God's grace, for His glory. You will not be a spiritual person only when the mood strikes you; your faith will remain constant in spite of your fluctuating emotions. Living for Christ means committing your spirit, soul and body to Him.

If you live for Christ, He will be alive to you and you will know the ecstasy of a life poured out before God as a thank-offering. Accept the gift of Himself in your life and allow Him to live through you. Then for you, to live is Christ and to die is gain.

Holy Jesus, live in me so that I will do
all things for Your glory. Amen.

A Growing Spirit

Your faith is growing more and more, and the love
every one of you has for each other is increasing.

2 THESSALONIANS 1:3

If you are not enjoying your spiritual experience, you have probably allowed stagnation to rob you of your spiritual zest.

A vibrant and powerful spiritual life requires constant attention. There will never be a point when nothing more is required from you. The longer you walk with the Lord, the greater your enthusiasm should be, and any tendency to grow slack should be resisted with all your might.

Your quiet times sustain and nurture your spiritual life. When you start fading spiritually, ask God for the wisdom and courage to confess your negligence and weakness and to help you do something constructive about it.

Lord, You who are the True Vine, let me grow in You
so that I can bear fruit that will please You. Amen.

A Balanced Inner Life

*If any of you lacks wisdom, he should ask God,
who gives generously to all without finding
fault, and it will be given to him.*

JAMES 1:5

Many people believe that to live a truly spiritual life, you need to live in seclusion; where the realities of life are either ignored or forgotten.

However, the lessons Jesus taught along the dusty roads of Palestine were very spiritual, yet essentially practical. For Him, everything – every thought and deed – was an expression of His relationship with His heavenly Father. Therefore, true Christians do not divide their lives into compartments, because all of their lives should be an expression of the spiritual.

Christianity touches the realities of every day and enables you to look, to a certain extent, at other people's problems as God does.

*O Spirit, take control of my life and let everything I do
and say be an expression of my love for You. Amen.*

Growth through Truth

*Like newborn babies, crave pure spiritual milk,
so that by it you may grow up in your salvation.*

1 PETER 2:2

If you ignore or undermine the necessity of growth in your spiritual life, it will not be long before you start to suffer on the stormy seas of disappointment and despair. There must be growth and development or your spiritual life will flounder on the rocks.

God makes resources available to us to assist us in our spiritual growth, such as fellowship with believers, Bible study and good deeds, but we should guard against these aids becoming goals in themselves. These are simply the result of our relationship with God and can never be a substitute for our faith in Him.

There can only be spiritual growth if your main objective is to reflect the image of Christ more and more. This should be the heart's desire of every believing Christian disciple.

My Lord, let Your Holy Spirit take possession of me so that I will live for Your glory alone. Amen.

Christlikeness

What will be has not yet been made known. But we know that when He appears, we shall be like Him.

1 JOHN 3:2

The goal of every Christian should be to become like Jesus. Unconditionally accepting the lordship of Christ is the beginning of a new and satisfying way of life. Because you belong to Him, your love and mental and spiritual energy should be focused on becoming like Him.

Of course trying to do this in your own strength will only lead to frustration and disappointment. Pray that God will give you His Holy Spirit to help you with this process.

When you are united with Him, your faith becomes alive and your whole life is lived in total obedience to Him. Having a dynamic faith and obeying Christ will help you develop a Christlike character.

Master, I ask that You would fill me with Your life and goodness so that I can be completely obedient to You in all things. Amen.

Maturity

*Until we all reach unity in the faith and in the knowledge
of the Son of God, and become mature, attaining
to the whole measure of the fullness of Christ.*

EPHESIANS 4:13

It takes time for intellectual and spiritual maturity to reach its full potential.

In your efforts to reach maturity, you should have something against which to measure your progress. The apostle Paul teaches that we should measure our progress against nothing less than the character of Christ. Although this is an impossible goal, to aim any lower is to accept a secondhand life.

However, never forget Jesus' love for you and that He identifies with you in your human frailty. God will give you the strength to lead a godly life if you confess your dependence on Him every moment of the day. Draw daily from the strength that He makes available to you.

*Through Your strength, Master and Savior,
I can aim to follow in Your steps. Amen.*

Let Others See Christ in You

He said to them, "Go into all the world and
preach the good news to all creation."

MARK 16:15

Christians need to be witnesses for Christ.
We must not be ashamed of our faith in Jesus
Christ. It is, however, important to know when
to speak and when to be quiet.

There is one sure way to testify about your
faith without offending other people, and that is
to follow the example of Jesus Christ. His whole
life was a testimony of commitment to His duty,
sympathy, mercy, and love for all people – regardless of their rank or circumstances. This is
the very best way to be a witness for Jesus.

Ask the Holy Spirit to guide you so that others will see Christ in everything you do and
say. In this way you will fulfill the command
of the Lord.

*Help me, Lord Jesus, to let the Holy Spirit live
through me in such a way that others may
know of Your love for them. Amen.*

Spiritual Growth through Prayer

*After Job had prayed for his friends,
the LORD made him prosperous again and
gave him twice as much as he had before.*

JOB 42:10

It is not hard to make enemies. But remember, it is always possible to turn an enemy into a friend – although this isn't easy, as forgiveness requires true greatness.

Only those who have undergone meaningful spiritual growth can transform enmity into friendship. One sure and practical way to turn enemies into friends is to pray for them. This may sound absurd but it is a truly wise act if you desire a pleasant life. Prayer changes your attitude toward people and events, and when this happens, the battle is just about won. With God on your side you will have the ultimate victory.

Dear Lord, help me to grow in You so that I may develop a forgiving spirit. You have forgiven me through Your grace. Help me to follow Your example. Amen.

Stand by Your Convictions

Simon Peter answered, "You are the Christ,
the Son of the living God."

MATTHEW 16:16

Many people long for a stronger faith. At one point or another we all need to answer the question that Jesus asked Simon Peter, "What about you? Who do you say I am?"

To benefit fully from the Christian experience, and to know the fullness and abundance of the true life that Jesus offers us, you must have a personal knowledge of the living Christ. This does not only mean learning everything about Him; it means acknowledging Him personally and surrendering your life to Him.

Acknowledge Christ's sovereignty over all creation and abundant life will be yours. That is why Jesus came to this world.

Make me a prisoner of Your love, O Lord,
because only then will I be truly free. Amen.

The Power of
Inspired Thoughts

Above all else, guard your heart,
for it is the wellspring of life.

PROVERBS 4:23

Our thoughts control our lives. If your spirit harbors thoughts of bitterness, hate and envy, your mind will be drenched with negative and destructive thoughts, and you will never experience the dynamism of the Christian faith.

By living in harmony with the living Christ, and allowing His Spirit to become an inspiration to your spirit, you can achieve the impossible. Embrace God's ways with joy, build a healthy and profound prayer life and engage in faithful Bible study. This will give your mind the inspiration and strength that is only experienced by those who have put Jesus Christ first in their lives.

Through Your enabling grace, Lord Jesus, my mind is
open to the inspiration of the Holy Spirit. Amen.

I Long for Your Commands

Your statutes are wonderful; therefore I obey them.
The unfolding of Your words gives light. Direct my
footsteps according to Your word; let no sin rule over me.

PSALM 119:129–130, 133

There are times in life when we long for guidance; long for someone who clearly knows the road ahead, who can help us avoid the potholes and dead-end streets.

This is the kind of desire that the psalmist had for the Word of God – that it would lead him every step of the way. He knew that the Word would lead him to true joy.

In today's world it often seems easier to desire God's freedom than His commandments. But the psalmist understood that God's commandments would bring true joy to his life.

Reaffirm your desire for God's Word to be your guide through life, today. Pray that God will help you resist the specific sins that cause you to stumble often.

*Lord of the Word, let Your commandments
guide me in the right paths. Amen.*

Nourish Your Soul

"I am the bread of life. He who comes to Me
will never go hungry, and he who believes
in Me will never be thirsty."

JOHN 6:35

In order to achieve a healthy existence and meet
the demands of everyday life, food is essential.

Just as your physical body needs nourishment, so too does your spiritual life. It is an
important and integral part of your existence
on earth, as well as in eternity. Make sure that
you maintain a sustained conversation with
Christ so that you can constantly draw on the
strength flowing from His everlasting reserves.

In this way you will ensure that your life
will be powerfully enriched, because Jesus is
living inside you through His Holy Spirit.

*Lord, You are my daily bread and Your truth sets
me free. Thank You for presenting us with the
Word so that we may get to know You better.
Help me to find You therein. Amen.*

Reach for the Sky!

*I want to know Christ and the power of His resurrection
and the fellowship of sharing in His sufferings,
becoming like Him in His death, and so, somehow,
to attain to the resurrection from the dead.*

PHILIPPIANS 3:10–11

Ambition is a commendable characteristic but there is one ideal in life that must overshadow all others: to live in the image of Christ. This must be the greatest ambition of every follower of Jesus and demands complete surrender and commitment

The pure joy of a life in Jesus Christ cannot be measured. Such a life is priceless and precious. However, this demands a sacrifice. A sacrifice of your thoughts and ambitions must be laid on the altar of the living Christ so that His life can be reflected in you. The abundance of life in Him will be more than enough compensation for your complete surrender to your Savior and Redeemer.

*Lord, I want to follow You and devote
my entire life to Your service. Amen.*

Stand by Your Convictions

"Blessed are you when men hate you, when they
exclude you and insult you and reject your name as evil,
because of the Son of Man. Rejoice in that day and
leap for joy, because great is your reward in heaven."

LUKE 6:22-23

There are a number of people who do not remain true to their principles and instead bow to societal pressure, suppressing their ideals.

If you do this, you violate your God-created character. What you believe is of crucial importance and becomes the only way for you to achieve true freedom in life.

If you are true to yourself, you may be scorned and rejected, but you will enjoy the satisfaction of knowing that you do not live a double life. It is only when you are at peace with yourself, and when you strive to please God rather than your fellow man, that you will be able to live a life of quality and contentment.

*Bless our labor in You, Lord. Help us to be steadfast
and strong, filled with fervor towards You. Amen.*

Grow in Wisdom
by Serving God

The fear of the Lord is the beginning of wisdom; all who follow His precepts have good understanding.

PSALM 111:10

To be educated is definitely an advantage in life. However, you can be highly educated and still suffer from spiritual want.

For the Christian, sanctification must always receive priority over education. A person who is in the process of developing spiritually is closer to the heart of God and, therefore, he is more skilled in understanding God's ways.

A spiritual person has discovered the true Source of wisdom in life. There is purpose in his service to God. He possesses peace and inner strength born from the fellowship of the Holy Spirit, and lives his life in such a way that he gains deep-rooted contentment and inspiration from it.

Lord, help me to spend every day in fellowship with you and to experience the fullness of life. Amen.

Spiritual Growth
Does Not Come Naturally

*The mind of sinful man is death, but the mind
controlled by the Spirit is life and peace.*

ROMANS 8:6

Physical growth is nature's way of allowing your body to develop. Your spiritual nature needs to grow too. Many people ignore this important aspect of their lives because it cannot be observed or measured like your body can. Yet, that does not make it any less important.

The greatest Guide and Advisor that you could ever find is Jesus Christ. He is the revelation of the living God and therefore has a perfect understanding of the problems that you wrestle with. Having a desire for oneness with Christ and yearning for a deeper relationship with Him will result in spiritual growth if you surrender to God completely.

I can do nothing without You. In You I can grow and gain fulfillment. I wish to remain in You always. Amen.

Spiritual Renewal
Is Essential

*He renews my strength. He guides me along
right paths, bringing honor to His name.*

PSALM 23:3 (NLT)

From time to time it is necessary to take a break in order to refresh yourself and prevent burnout. Jesus often withdrew Himself from the masses and from society so that He could be alone with His Father.

It is even more necessary for us to spend time with our heavenly Father. It is in those precious moments when you spend quiet time with God, that you will discover the work of the Holy Spirit in your life. He will fill the empty reservoirs of your life and you will return to the world refreshed, bearing testimony of Him with the new strength and energy that you have drawn from the Source.

*Lord, fill me with Your Spirit. I ask for comfort,
strength and guidance – all to Your glory. Amen.*

Reflect God's Glory

Be imitators of God, therefore, as dearly loved children.

EPHESIANS 5:1

Most of us have a role model to which we aspire to be like, whether it is a teacher, a parent, an employer or even a friend, we want to be like them.

Yet, there is a much better role model for us, a perfect role model for you and me – Jesus Christ. Never forget that He lived and worked just like us and was subject to all the temptations, frustrations, joys and sorrows to which you and I are subject to.

Allow the Holy Spirit to take control of your life and manage it in a way that is acceptable to God. Then you will display a measure of likeness to Christ that will glorify God.

Lord, transform me into Your image more and more. Transfigure me so that I may become more like You in my behavior, thoughts and words. Amen.

The Most
Important Exercise

"The good man brings good things out of the good
stored up in his heart, and the evil man brings evil
things out of the evil stored up in his heart.
For out of the overflow of his heart his mouth speaks."

LUKE 6:45

It is the quality of your inner life, not that
which you pretend to be, that is significant. For
a while you may be able to present a false front,
but a time will come when storm clouds gather
and you will be put to the test.

Cultivating a practical spiritual life is the
most important exercise that one can undertake.
It influences every aspect of your life and creates moral stamina, which enables you to rise
victoriously above inner weaknesses.

When you live in harmony with God and
allow the Holy Spirit to work in you, you will
experience a motivating force in your life that
will be reflected in your behavior.

Lord, teach me to fix my eyes on You more and more.
I want to devote my whole life to You. Amen.

Aspire to That Which Is Noble

*Finally, brothers, whatever is true, whatever is noble,
whatever is right, whatever is pure, whatever is lovely,
whatever is admirable – if anything is excellent
or praiseworthy – think about such things.*

PHILIPPIANS 4:8

Life can be an unpleasant or an exquisite experience, depending on your attitude towards it. When you are confronted with the cruelty of life, it is all too easy to allow it to affect your nature and character.

It requires spiritual sensitivity to consistently appreciate the beauty of life. To appreciate God as the Creator of all that is beautiful and noble, look around you. You will discover Him in unexpected places: in the smile of a friend, the innocence of a child, even a subtle act of love. In numerous ways, you will begin to see the wonder and beauty of life.

*I bring You humble thanks, O Savior, that through
the presence of Your Spirit I can appreciate
the beauty and grandeur of life. Amen.*

Share in the Life of Christ

God, who has called you into fellowship with
His Son Jesus Christ our Lord, is faithful.

1 CORINTHIANS 1:9

God has called you to share in the life of His Son, Jesus the living Christ – granting us a privilege beyond words.

But with this privilege comes responsibilities. Intimacy with the Father demands that the holy characteristics of God must be revealed in your daily life by love, honesty, selflessness and the integrity of your purpose. If you walk in the truth of this amazing grace, your understanding of God deepens and your vision of what your life could be broadens.

Once you have this you will never again be limited by secret fears and doubts. Instead you will face the future with confidence in the strength of the living Christ.

You are the True Vine that gives lasting life.
Keep me safe, inspire me and bless me so that
I will forever remain fruitful. Amen.

The Person
You Can Become

*However, as it is written: "No eye has seen,
no ear has heard, no mind has conceived what
God has prepared for those who love Him."*

1 CORINTHIANS 2:9

There are two sides to your personality: the person you are, and the person you would like to be. If these are in conflict with each other, you will experience bitter frustration and disappointment.

There is no harm in dreaming about the heights that you can achieve, provided that you take steps to make your dream a reality. You have the potential for spiritual growth that is beyond your wildest imaginings.

Spiritual greatness can be yours if you live in harmony with God. Your whole life should respond to His love with joy and gratitude.

*I pray for inspiration and strength to become all that
You created me to be. Help me to grow in You day by
day and to fulfill Your vision for my life. Amen.*

In the Service of God

*Do your best to present yourself to God as one approved,
a workman who does not need to be ashamed and
who correctly handles the word of truth.*

2 TIMOTHY 2:15

Some people work tirelessly for God, seldom leaving any free time for themselves. Have you become so involved in God's work that you've lost sight of what God wants you to do?

If you don't get "topped up" by God regularly, one day something will just wither in your soul, all Christian activities will cease, and a life that may have been of great importance to God is lost.

The most important duty of any Christian worker is to strengthen your relationship with God every day. If you are too busy to spend time with Him in daily prayer then you are simply too busy to be an effective servant for the Almighty God.

*Loving Master, help me not to lose sight of
the service You want me to do. Amen.*

Renew Your Character

Therefore, if anyone is in Christ, he is a new
creation; the old has gone, the new has come!

2 CORINTHIANS 5:17

Most people observe our characters and form
an impression based on what they see. Yet,
only a few people take the time to develop an
agreeable character.

Many people believe that a person's character cannot be changed. This is not true. If this
were so, the redeeming love of Christ would
have been in vain. Sinners can change into saints
and unpleasant people can become amiable
when the love of Christ enters their hearts.

When you open your life to Christ, His influence is reflected in your life and a transfor-
mation occurs. You surrender yourself to the
Lord and through that, your character changes.

*Your love is always with me, Lord. Father, draw
me closer into Your circle of love every day.
I want to remain in You. Amen.*

june

PEACE IN GOD

It Is Well with My Soul

*Why have you rejected us forever, O God? Why does
Your anger smolder against the sheep of Your pasture?*

PSALM 74:1

There are many people whose lives fall apart, and they feel abandoned and forsaken. Yet it is not true to believe that God will ever forsake you. He has promised to be with you always and to never leave you (Heb. 13:5). He even proved His unfathomable love by sacrificing His only Son on the cross for us.

God has a divine purpose for everything that happens in your life. Even when you are the victim of adversity, don't despair. He wants to use these circumstances to bring about His perfect will in your life.

*Be still, my soul, the Lord is on your side. Patiently
bear all sorrow and grief and leave all decisions in
His loving hands. When everything else fails,
You, Lord, remain faithful. Amen.*

Light in the Darkness

To those who have been called, who are loved
by God the Father and kept by Jesus Christ:
Mercy, peace and love be yours in abundance.

JUDE 1-2

It seems as if the world is in a perpetual state of chaos. Lawlessness and violence are increasing, and people live in fear and insecurity. What is the solution to such a sad state of affairs?

There can only be one answer and that is to turn to Jesus Christ. He has already conquered this dark and hostile world and replaced fear with love so that You can confidently place your faith and trust in Him.

Believe in Jesus and His promises and He will give you the blessing of His peace that transcends all understanding. Trust in Him and He will lead you from the darkness into the light of His immeasurable love for us.

Thank You, my Lord and God, that You grant perfect peace to Your children in this dark world. Amen.

God Is with You

*"The Lord your God is with you, He is mighty to save.
He will take great delight in you."*

ZEPHANIAH 3:17

When things go wrong in life it is easy to despair and become overwhelmed by a sense of complete helplessness and hopelessness.

If ever anything seemed hopeless, it was on the day of Jesus' crucifixion. The hopes and dreams of those who thought that He was the promised Messiah were shattered when He died on the cross. But then God intervened and miraculously turned apparent defeat into victory. The sorrowful Good Friday was transformed into the triumphant resurrection of the Easter Sunday – when Christ rose victoriously from the grave.

Whatever circumstances you might find yourself in, however dismal, always remember that God is with you and that He is in control of your circumstances.

*Redeemer and Friend, thank You that I can be sure
that God loves me and is always with me. Amen.*

Peace and Prosperity

You will keep in perfect peace him whose
mind is steadfast, because he trusts in You.

ISAIAH 26:3

When our minds are focused on the love of
God, we experience indescribable tranquility
and peace of mind. When you trust God during every day, and through every problem,
you will be able to enjoy His peace.

By focusing on Jesus Christ and the peace
and prosperity that He gives, you are set free
from worry because you know that God is in
control of your life – therefore no person or
circumstance can disturb your tranquility.

His love enfolds you and covers your loved
ones as well. This freedom cannot be taken away
by anyone or anything – simply because you put
your trust in the Lord.

*I want to trust You with every aspect of my life
because of Your great love. Then my heart will be
filled with peace and I will fear no evil. Amen.*

Constructive Service

Being confident of this very thing, that He
who has begun a good work in you will
complete it until the day of Jesus Christ.

PHILIPPIANS 1:6 (NKJV)

From every generation Jesus Christ has His followers who preach His gospel and do His will. Some of them reach high positions in society; others perform the task He has assigned to them to the best of their ability. One thing that the followers of Christ should understand is that the Master comes to them in their own, unique circumstances.

As your relationship with Jesus Christ deepens, you will be guided into constructive service. You become aware of a divine plan unfolding for your life. Such a plan might perhaps not be dramatic, but it is God's plan for you, and in executing it you will find joy and a deep satisfaction – as well as His protection.

Master, make my experience with You one that will
take me to higher heights in my walk with You. Amen.

Your Will Be Done

"Yet not My will, but Yours be done."

LUKE 22:42

Many things come our way in life – unexpected disappointments and trials – and often we cannot see any reason for them. But whether they are major or minor problems, we need to handle them all.

The Lord's love for us is endlessly tender and encouraging. He wants us to trust where we cannot see, and it will not be a reckless leap in the dark, as sincere trust and faith says, "I know for certain that God's will is best for me." This kind of faith leaves the choice up to God, with the words His Son taught us, "Your will be done!"

Eternal God and Father, thank You for sending
Your Son to come and teach me what it means
to let Your will be done in my life. Let
Your Spirit assist me in this. Amen.

Through Him
Who Strengthens Me

*Blessed is the man who trusts in the LORD,
whose confidence is in Him.*

JEREMIAH 17:7

Everybody is searching for peace. No one can avoid the strain of life or the severe stress it brings with it. Jesus radiated love, serenity and peace; no matter how turbulent or chaotic the circumstances were around Him.

This was the result of His intimate relationship with His Father. Jesus regularly withdrew in solitude to pray and pour out His heart to His Father. Then He was able to return to a stormy life with the peace of heaven in His heart.

Whatever life may have in store for you, you will be victorious in His strength because, "I can do everything through Him who gives me strength" (Phil. 4:13).

*You are my Keeper, O Lord. I place myself under
Your control and in Your care. That is why
I am assured of Your peace. Amen.*

The Great Comfort

He comforts us in all our troubles
so that we can comfort others.

2 CORINTHIANS 1:4 (NLT)

Paul had first-hand knowledge of the Father's compassion during his trials. He learnt that God is "the source of all comfort" and comforts us in any circumstance (see 2 Cor. 1:3). This comfort flows directly from our fellowship with God.

It often happens that our own sorrow is relieved while we comfort others. Our hearts become sensitive to others because of the trials and sorrow we have wrestled with ourselves. That is why there is a blessing in every burden and affliction in our lives. We must simply receive the grace through the Holy Spirit to see it and share it with others. In so doing, our own sorrow is toned down and we are able to reach out to others with a comforting hand and heart.

*Holy Comforter, let Your healing love
enfold my heart so that I will be tender
in my contact with others' grief. Amen.*

Peace Amidst Chaos

In keeping with His promise we are looking forward to a new heaven and a new earth, the home of righteousness.

2 PETER 3:13

In times of crises many people tend to collapse in defeat against what they perceive to be impossible problems. But to everyone who believes in Him, Jesus offers a life of abundance.

The Lord offers you His Holy Spirit if you surrender yourself to Him. It is His Spirit who gives you the ability to handle life's problems successfully. Whatever your circumstances may be, remember that Jesus is constantly at your side, guiding you and helping you. Place your trust in Him as He leads you, and remember that He is guiding you toward God's kingdom where there is only harmony and peace.

Beloved Guide, I know that this life's struggles and problems will soon pass, and then I will enter into the eternal peace of Your kingdom. Amen.

Peace in the Storm

While they were still talking about this,
Jesus Himself stood among them
and said to them, "Peace be with you."

LUKE 24:36

The stress, horror and inner conflict we may experience in life causes our peace to disappear, leaving us moody and discontent.

That is why we need to develop inner reserves from which to draw strength in difficult situations. When things go wrong and stress starts to overwhelm you, purposefully refuse to be swept into its current. Guard against bad temper and irritability.

Deliberately choose to remain tranquil by controlling your thoughts. Spend some time in God's presence, reaffirm your dependence on Him, and soon your spirit will become calm and His peace will refresh your life.

Eternal God who gives me peace in Jesus Christ,
lead me to quiet waters where there is peace
in the midst of the bustle of life. Amen.

I Know for Certain

He will never leave you nor forsake you.

DEUTERONOMY 31:6

It is important to have someone you can rely on and turn to in times of trouble. Yet sometimes even the closest friends can disappoint you.

Our Lord and Master will never let us down, however. If you need comfort, the Lord will comfort you. If you need guidance, the Lord will guide you. If you need inspiration for a difficult task, the Lord will inspire you.

If the road ahead of you seems to be strewn with problems, concerns and troubles, then ask the Lord to help you and you will discover that He is as faithful as His Word promises.

God my Father, thank You that I have the assurance
that You will never leave me nor forsake me.
Forgive me for the times when I've failed
and disappointed You. Amen.

Take Your Worries to God

"Therefore do not worry about tomorrow,
for tomorrow will worry about itself.
Each day has enough trouble of its own."

MATTHEW 6:34

Many people like to sit and brood over their problems. If we do this, we allow worry to flourish and then we lose hope.

Write down your worries clearly and simply. Then calmly pray about each one and scale them down to their real size. Prayerfully confirm that God is in control of every situation and that worry will no longer affect your tranquility and peace of mind.

The secret is to take your burdens to God in prayer. If you take this step today you will discover that you are prohibiting worry and anxiety from clouding your future because you will discover that Christ is all-sufficient for your needs, today and tomorrow.

Savior, I praise and thank You that You protect
me and lead me into a pleasant future. Amen.

Peace in the Storm

Great peace have they who love Your law,
and nothing can make them stumble.

PSALM 119:165

If you allow your thoughts to dwell on the things that are happening in the world today, you run the risk of being caught up in a whirlpool of hatred, bitterness and fear.

Yet, when your faith threatens to falter, God gives you the power to believe that all things will work out for the good of those who love Him. Peace is the direct result of trust. When your faith in God is sure, you receive an inner calm that brings balance to your life. Put God first in all things and you will know His peace and joy, even in the most trying circumstances.

Almighty God, thank You that with You at the center of my life I fear no storms, not even problems as threatening as hurricanes. Amen.

Heavenly Peace

"Peace I leave with you; My peace I give you."

JOHN 14:27

The peace that Jesus offers His followers differs from human peace and allows us to look at life through God's eyes. When we do this, the worldly things suddenly do not seem to be that important. What God thinks of you, and how you relate to God, forms the foundation for your peace.

We need His peace in our everyday lives as well as in our inner beings. The Lord does not want us to stress about what is happening around us. So in all the confusion and chaos of daily life, look away from the world and look up to God. He is waiting to grant us His peace and love.

Prince of Peace, thank You that I know for certain that You have not only redeemed me, but that You also grant me Your heavenly peace. Amen.

God's Peace Is Unfailing

Who is God besides the LORD?
And who is the Rock except our God?

2 SAMUEL 22:32

Often when people are experiencing problems, or if they need advice, they turn to a friend for help. But human effort always falls short.

If you find yourself in a difficult situation, don't underestimate the power and love of God. Complete healing flows from an absolute and unconditional trust in, and surrender to, the living Christ. It doesn't matter what your problem is, the only lasting solution is to be found in the unfathomable love which God, through Jesus, bestowed on humanity.

Never be too proud or too afraid to turn to Jesus. Lay all your problems at His feet. He gave His life for you and will grant you the healing balm of His peace.

I want to hold on to You, Lord, when the storm winds blow and I feel insecure. Grant me Your peace. Amen.

Peace Be with You!

For the sake of my brothers and friends,
I will say, "Peace be within you."

PSALM 122:8

The world has enough problems without us adding to them by engaging in bitter quarrels and harboring hurts against others. To enjoy life fully, it is essential that you live in peace with your fellow man – but you can only do that if you have peace within yourself.

During His earthly ministry, Jesus had to handle a tremendous amount of adversity and enmity. He endured mockery, hatred, humiliation, unfair criticism and rejection. But, He never allowed circumstances to get the better of Him.

This was only possible because He was at peace with God, with Himself, and with all people. Accept it and express it through your life and you will experience a life of harmony and peace.

Savior, because I found You, my life is filled
with an indescribable peace. Amen.

The Center of Christ's Peace

*The fruit of righteousness will be peace; the effect of
righteousness will be quietness and confidence forever.*

ISAIAH 32:17

Few people can honestly say that they do not
long for peace of mind and inner tranquility.
The troubles and pressures of life can drive
many to seek comfort in different things; be it
tranquilizers, drugs, professional help or even
alcohol. Others simply give in to despair and
just go through the motions of life.

The only proven way to handle the problems
and tensions of life is by having a faith that is
steadfastly grounded in the living Christ. Hold
on to Him in all circumstances, talk to Him
and, regardless of how desperate your situation might be, trust that He is always with you.
His peace will then fill your heart, helping you
overcome all your fears.

*Prince of Peace, please help me to turn to You first
in everything that happens to me today. Amen.*

Your Search for Peace

*To whom He said, "This is the resting place,
let the weary rest"; and, "This is the place
of repose" — but they would not listen.*

ISAIAH 28:12

People today struggle with tremendous pressure and in such stressful times tend to become very weary.

That is why Christ invites us by saying, "Come to Me, all you who are weary and burdened, and I will give you rest" (Matt. 11:28). Yet, instead of accepting this offer, many of us still try to find man-made solutions to our problems in our own strength.

Regardless of how busy you are, you must make time to withdraw from the demands of the day and spend time quietly at the feet of the Master. Focus on Him and His love. Regardless of how demanding and frantic your life may be, in the quietness you will be strengthened by God's peace.

*I have such a need for Your rest, Lord. Help me to be
strengthened in the peace of Your presence. Amen.*

Freedom and Peace in Christ

Jesus replied, "I tell you the truth,
everyone who sins is a slave to sin."

JOHN 8:34

Many people are slaves to destructive habits and lead sinful lives that are devoid of beauty and liberty.

Unfortunately many people have accepted this bondage as a way of life. They are content to live an inferior spiritual life because they are oblivious to the freedom and peace that Christ offers.

When you accept Christ as your Lord, you enjoy a new freedom, and a new pattern of life begins. All bitterness dissipates in His glorious love. The Holy Spirit sanctifies your thoughts, words and actions. The freedom that Christ gives spans your whole life and is the only way to find freedom and joy.

By doing Your will, Father, my life will be filled with a peace that lasts forever. Amen.

Christ's Peace –
My Inheritance

"In Me you may have peace. In this world
you will have trouble. But take heart!
I have overcome the world."

JOHN 16:33

This world's peace is a poor reflection of the peace that God gives to His children. The peace of God is the most wonderful peace imaginable. It affects every area of our lives. It is constant and does not change according to our moods.

But this peace requires a steadfast faith in Jesus Christ, who is the source of this peace. Such peace banishes worry, because that is the weapon the devil uses to undermine our peace. Jesus prohibits fear, because fear is the enemy of all peace.

I praise and thank You for the peace that conquers the fear and anxiety in my life. Amen.

God's Perfect Timing

"I am the Lord; in its time I will do this swiftly."

ISAIAH 60:22

Very often we find it difficult to accept God's timing, but we must never get impatient with the fact that He does not always react when we want Him too.

It is wrong to try to subject the omniscient God to your timetable. We only see the circumstances and problems that weigh us down now, while God sees the bigger picture from an eternal perspective. God's timing is always perfect, even though it may not seem that way to you now.

When His will becomes our primary concern, then we will start to understand God's perfect timing and will no longer be subject to fits of anxiety caused by circumstances.

Lord, You are omnipresent. When I lose all hope,
You are there. Thank You that I may know
that my life is safe in Your hands. Amen.

God Enables You To Control Your Thoughts

Let the peace of Christ rule in your hearts,
since as members of one body you were called to peace.

COLOSSIANS 3:15

Your thoughts are your servant. Your thoughts influence your deeds because what you think and believe is the result of your circumstances. It is therefore imperative to discipline your thoughts in order to have a positive and constructive disposition towards life.

The greatest force in a healthy and emotional life is allowing the Holy Spirit to take control of your thoughts. You can, through the strength that Christ grants you, control your thoughts, and in doing so, experience the peace of God. There will be moments of disruption when evil thoughts will try to re-establish themselves, but if you focus on God and give Him control, nothing will destroy your peace.

You are my only Savior. Help me to trust in God as my shield against the Evil One. Amen.

The Blessing of a Peacemaker

"Blessed are the peacemakers, for they will be called sons of God."

MATTHEW 5:9

Peacemakers create healthy relationships. They are people in whose presence bitterness, hatred and unforgiveness simply cannot survive. They are children of God and aim to be at peace with all people.

To live in peace with friends is easy, but what about your enemies? Therefore it is peace at a risk: it includes peace with your enemies and persecutors.

Peacemakers are willing to venture something so that they can perform a deed of peace for the sake of Christ. To be a peacemaker is not a pious ideal or an unreachable dream; in Christ, it is an achievable goal through the help of the Holy Spirit.

Holy Spirit of God, enable me, for the sake of Jesus, my Lord, to be a peacemaker in this world. Amen.

In His Safekeeping

He led His own people like a flock of sheep,
guiding them safely through the wilderness.
He kept them safe so they were not afraid.

PSALM 78:52–53 (NLT)

On a spiritual level, a life of doubt, anxiety and fear without any peace of mind can become a real nightmare. If you want peace of mind and tranquility to become a reality in your life, it is of the essence that you cling to your faith in Jesus with all your might.

Believe in His promise that He will always be with you and never let you down (see Heb. 13:5). Go to Him with every situation that makes you anxious and trust Him to protect you against all fear, anxiety and evil. Then you will experience the peace of God.

Place yourself in God's safekeeping now and forever. He will keep you safe.

Protect me, Lord, in all circumstances and keep me safe so that I will overcome my fear. Amen.

Green Pastures

He makes me lie down in green pastures,
He leads me beside quiet waters.

PSALM 23:2

It is a blessed assurance to know that an omnipotent and loving God guides you from day to day. The Lord does not promise that all the pastures will always be green – sometimes they will be barren and desolate. He has also not promised that the waters will always be tranquil – sometimes the waves will break turbulently over us and the sky will be covered with ominous storm clouds. But the promise is that God, in His time, will bring us to green pastures and quiet waters.

If we put our childlike and unconditional trust in Him, we may rest assured in the knowledge that God will guide us in our everyday lives.

Lord Jesus, Shepherd of my life, thank You that
I may be safe and secure in Your care. Help me
to accept Your guidance at all times. Amen.

The Lord Guides Us

Then the disciple whom Jesus loved
said to Peter, "It is the Lord!"

JOHN 21:7

When the disciples beached at dawn following a night of fishing, they recognized Jesus on the shore. He had prepared a meal for them. This tells us of the Lord's care – even after His resurrection He stayed close to His children.

We will get rid of a multitude of anxieties and confusions if we only recognize the Lord's hand in our lives and know for certain that He is by our side in every situation.

We know that He guides us on the path that is best for us. If we meet Jesus with unfailing certainty every day on our path through life, then we are amongst the most fortunate of all people on earth.

I praise and glorify You, Lord Jesus, because I see Your hand in every situation in my life and I know for certain that You will never forsake me. Amen.

God Is the Source of Peace

*I pray that God, the source of hope,
will fill you completely with joy and
peace because you trust in Him.*

ROMANS 15:13 (NLT)

Peace of mind is the quiet but certain knowledge that you are secure in God's care. When I accept God as the Source of my peace and joy, and I become inseparably united with Him, I have taken the first step on the road to peace. When my spirit is in peaceful harmony with God, I live in harmony and peace with my fellow humans.

Few things can destroy peace of mind as completely as strife in your relationship with God and those around you. To remedy this situation, our relationship with God needs to be strengthened through Jesus Christ and the Holy Spirit. The wonder of God's peace is one of the "perks" of a surrendered life. The condition for this is faith.

*Merciful Father, thank You that I can draw
near to You, the source of true peace. Amen.*

Shelter from the Storm

He who dwells in the shelter of the Most High
will rest in the shadow of the Almighty.
I will say of the LORD, "He is my refuge
and my fortress, my God, in whom I trust."

PSALM 91:1-2

Our lives can only be safe if we trust in the Most
High. His protection is not limited to certain
times of the day; rather we are under God's
protection every moment of the night and day.

You need not fear anything – not the dangers of night or the attacks of day, not illness
and plague, nor war and fighting. God is with
us everywhere – at home, on the roads, even in
the workplace. With His protection and presence you will be able to conquer all dangers.

Take shelter under God's wings and be assured that you have a safe refuge where true
peace and safety can be found.

*God of Ages, Your children have always
found shelter and protection in You.
Thank You that I know for certain that I will
also find it when I come to You. Amen.*

Feast of Peace

*"I am leaving you with a gift – peace of mind and heart.
And the peace I give is a gift the world cannot
give. So don't be troubled or afraid."*

JOHN 14:27 (NLT)

In a world that is so chaotic and conflicted, it seems naively idealistic to talk about peace. But peace is one of the gifts that God offers us through Jesus Christ. It is an eternal truth that all who love and serve God will experience His peace in their personal lives.

For those who have God's peace, it does not mean that they will escape the problems and sorrows of life, it means that they possess something more precious than the spirit of the times in which we live.

Christ's peace is not a passive quality that shuts our eyes to the harsh reality, but creates a positive approach to life, based on the belief in the trustworthiness of God.

*Praise the Lord! Jesus, You came to bring peace.
Thank You for the peace of this glorious
truth ruling in my own heart. Amen.*

Relieve Anxiety

An anxious heart weighs a man down,
but a kind word cheers him up.

PROVERBS 12:25

In times of pressure and stress – when it feels as if hope is dying – anxiety takes root in your heart and mind and flourishes. Anxiety is the product of a confused mind and little faith.

One way of overcoming a feeling of anxiety is to determine its cause. For many people their anxiety is vague and indefinable, but it continues to erode their spirit and mind – with disastrous consequences. Take your anxieties to God and ask Him to be Master of the situation. If you do this, you are no longer allowing the Devil to attack your calm approach to life or allowing anxiety to spoil tomorrow.

Holy Spirit of God, help me not to be anxious
about tomorrow, because You have every day
in Your eternal and loving hand. Amen.

july

HOPE AND TRUST

A New Hope

Trust in the LORD with all your heart and lean
not on your own understanding; in all your ways
acknowledge Him, and He will make your paths straight.

PROVERBS 3:5-6

The decisions you make on a daily basis could have far-reaching consequences for your life. Spend some time in God's presence today and seek His will. This will lay a solid foundation for a life built on trust in the living Christ.

God will never disappoint you. Through the Holy Spirit, He will open up new horizons of what life can offer. Your values will change as you start looking at life through His eyes.

The more closely you walk with Him, the more clearly you will understand all that He can do in and through your life. Resolve to strengthen and enrich your relationship with Christ so that you can blossom and be as fruitful as He desires you to be.

*Loving Lord, I come before You in earnest
prayer, asking that my imperfect life might
reflect something of Your holiness. Amen.*

Hope for the Future

*Has He not made with me an everlasting covenant,
arranged and secured in every part?*

2 SAMUEL 23:5

Many people look to the future with deep anxiety because they are carrying the heavy burden of their daily responsibilities alone. Unless you have a strong faith, this could have far-reaching effects on your physical, emotional and mental well-being.

The Son of the Most High God died and rose from the dead to set you free from this burden of worry. God loved you so much that Jesus Christ gave His life to redeem you from the terrible burden of anxious worries. Unlike those who have no hope, you are blessed with the assurance that the Savior died in order that you may live. Regardless of the circumstances you're in, this assurance should be a great comfort and encouragement.

*I thank You, Lord, that in spite of my
circumstances I can praise You, for You are
in control and You are ever-faithful. Amen.*

Living Hope

Praise be to the God and Father of our Lord
Jesus Christ! In His great mercy He has given
us new birth into a living hope through the
resurrection of Jesus Christ from the dead.

1 PETER 1:3

Let your anxious heart rejoice with the glorious expectations of all the riches and treasures that await you in heaven. Thank God for such a hope and turn your thoughts away from all the burdens and worries of the world. Renew your mind with thoughts of the pure untainted inheritance that is waiting for you – an inheritance that can never be destroyed.

Prayer focuses our hearts on heaven while our feet remain firmly planted on the earth. So even if you are involved in a bitter struggle here on earth, remember your inheritance in heaven and praise the Lord.

I thank and praise You, Holy God, for all the treasures that You have set aside for me in heaven. Amen.

Trust God

I heard, but I did not understand. So I asked,
"My lord, what will the outcome of all this be?"

DANIEL 12:8

People often find it difficult to understand God's purpose for their lives – especially when things go wrong. Their vision of the future fades and their faith wavers.

The core of a strong faith depends on your ability to trust God completely, no matter what happens. The true test of faith comes when things turn against you; when you are tempted to question God; when you are in total despair.

Jesus had an unconditional trust in God. Even in His darkest moments, His faith was strong enough to enable Him to fulfill the will of the Father. Trust God in all circumstances and the grace of God will help you in every situation.

Lamb of God, I look up to You to strengthen my faith
through the work of Your Holy Spirit in my life. Amen.

Faith in God

*Though an army besiege me, my heart
will not fear; though war break out
against me, even then will I be confident.*

PSALM 27:3

Like never before, people are worried and anxious about what the future holds. It is essential for people to have a spiritual foundation upon which to base their hopes and expectations. Unless you have a positive trust in a power greater than yourself, the future will be filled with uncertainty for you.

Faith in God must be intimate and personal if it is to give you hope for the future. The omnipotent Creator God has not abandoned this world despite appearances to the contrary. His master plan will still be carried out, just place your trust in Him and meet the future with the serenity He will give you.

*Savior and Lord, I live from day to day trusting Your
very real presence and omnipotence in this world.
I do not fear because You are my refuge. Amen.*

On Eagles' Wings

Those who hope in the LORD will renew their strength.
They will soar on wings like eagles.

ISAIAH 40:31

Too often we get hung up on things that don't really matter and we allow them to distort our view of life.

A positive Christian, however, has the ability to rise above small irritations by trusting in the Lord in all circumstances and by always remaining conscious of His presence. It is impossible to be trivial and small-minded when the love of Christ fills your heart and mind.

Spreading God's love by the power of the Holy Spirit means being able to rise above trivialities and reach the heights that the God of love desires from all His children. Then we can rise up on the wings of eagles and see things from their true perspective.

Holy Spirit, fill me with Your presence and help me to trust in God so I can rise above my problems. Amen.

Unshakable Trust

Blessed is he whose help is the God of Jacob,
whose hope is in the Lᴏʀᴅ his God.

PSALM 146:5

When everything seems to be going wrong you may feel overwhelmed by your problems and want to give up or try to solve them in your own strength. But remember, the Lord has promised to never leave nor forsake you.

However, you must have patience because you cannot hurry or prescribe to God. He does everything in His own perfect time and way. God sees the big picture of your life – He is all-knowing and all-seeing.

Pray and ask the Holy Spirit to teach you to wait patiently on the Lord. Then, you can leave everything in God's hands. Those who stand steadfast in affliction receive God's most precious gifts from His treasure house of mercy.

Lord and Father, I find peace of mind
in trusting You completely. Amen.

Holy and Omniscient

The Lord has established His throne in heaven,
and His kingdom rules over all.

PSALM 103:19

In adverse circumstances, people often start to doubt God's power and majesty. Their faith often wanes and the obstacles of life cause them to stumble.

When you find yourself surrounded by difficulties, hold on to your faith and put all your trust in the victorious Christ. In all the centuries since Creation, there has not been one instance where the righteousness of God did not triumph over evil.

This same God wants to be your daily companion. He reigns supremely over everything and everyone. Let this be your source of strength and power in life, with all its problems and demands.

*Father, I find strength and inspiration in
knowing that You are with me, and that Your
righteousness prevails in every situation. Amen.*

Facing the Future

I saw the Lord always before me. Because
He is at my right hand, I will not be shaken.
Therefore my heart is glad and my tongue rejoices;
my body also will live in hope.

ACTS 2:25–26

If you are fearful and worried about the future, you will project the very things that you fear and wish to avoid, into your future. Like Job you will then find yourself saying, "What I feared has come upon me" (Job 3:25).

A sure way of increasing your hope is to work hard at maintaining a positive faith in Jesus Christ. Strengthen the ties that you have with Him until He becomes a living, dynamic reality to you.

The more real He becomes to you, the more your fears, which have undermined your trust in Him, will be transformed into a steadfast, constant faith in the Lord. Then you will be able to venture fearlessly into the future.

*Holy Master, give me hope and confidence
in the future as I walk with You. Amen.*

Trust God in the Darkness

*Yea, though I walk through the valley of the shadow
of death, I will fear no evil; for You are with me;
Your rod and Your staff they comfort me.*

PSALM 23:4 (NKJV)

Every follower of Jesus faces days where his or her spiritual life seems mediocre and their enthusiasm is dampened by indifference.

If this is you, then you need a fresh experience with God to drive the darkness from your life. No matter how your feelings and emotions change, God's love for you remains steadfast, strong and secure. He loves you with an everlasting, unceasing love, and, even though you feel far from Him, He is always close to you.

One of the benefits of going through dark times in life is to appreciate the light and sunshine of God's love when we experience it once again. God is able to use even the darkest experiences on your earthly pilgrimage to the benefit and blessing of others.

*Please hold my hand, Lord. I know that You will
lead me into the future one step at a time. Amen.*

A Life Based on Trust

I have learnt to be content whatever the
circumstances. I know what it is to be in need,
and I know what it is to have plenty.

PHILIPPIANS 4:11–12

As a follower of Christ you have powers at your disposal that enable you to tackle life positively and constructively. Remember that dynamic discipleship is based on faith that finds expression in deeds, not in feelings. Focus on the fact that God loves you, even though you might be experiencing the darkest time of your life.

Acknowledge the fact that He will never leave you, even though you may not be able to feel His presence right now. If your life is based on your faith in Christ, your confidence will increase and you will overcome every feeling of inferiority. There will be no situation that you will not be able to handle through Christ's wisdom and power.

I thank You, Lord Jesus, that I can start every day with confidence because I find my strength in You. Amen.

Faith Requires Trust

"Master, we've worked hard all night and
haven't caught anything. But because
you say so, I will let down the nets."

LUKE 5:5

The disciples had labored hard throughout the night without catching any fish. They were experienced fishermen and knew there were no fish to catch. Yet, at Jesus' words, they let down the nets once more. According to the Scriptures they caught so many fish that the nets began to tear. And so their faith was rewarded.

When you lay a matter before God you should trust Him so much that you are willing to accept His will and be obedient to the prompting of His Spirit no matter what. Forget about what others think or say; trust God unconditionally and He will reward your faith.

I place my trust in You completely, Lord Jesus, in the knowledge that You will never disappoint me. Help me not to disappoint You through my unbelief. Amen.

Trust in God

Let us hold unswervingly to the hope we profess,
for He who promised is faithful.

HEBREWS 10:23

Sometimes everything in your life looks hopeless and bleak. Your dreams have been destroyed, your hope has died, and nothing seems to be working out right. In such a depressed state we become easy prey to the Devil, whose main aim is to drive a wedge between our heavenly Father and us.

When you feel dejected, remember that Jesus has promised to be by your side throughout your life. He invites you to cast your problems on Him and to trust Him in times of distress. Study the Gospels, see how compassionate and loving Jesus was towards people, and draw hope and comfort from that.

Thank You, Lord Jesus, that even when
I feel dejected, You are always by my side.
Lift me from the well of misery and let me
sing a song of praise once more. Amen.

The Richness of Life

Not that we are competent in ourselves to claim anything for ourselves, but our competence comes from God.

2 CORINTHIANS 3:5

If you are searching for the deeper meaning of life, you are on an exciting journey. Fix your eyes beyond the temporal, and discover that you are an eternal being created in God's image.

God gives purpose to your days and motivation to live life to the full. As you yield to the control of the Holy Spirit, you will become more and more aware of how magnificent life truly is.

If we would only surrender to God without restraint we would see His glory and omnipotence and we would experience the richness of life in all its facets.

Great and mighty God. I praise You for revealing Your greatness to me and enriching my life through it. Amen.

Peace through Jesus Christ

*He came and preached peace to you who were
far away and peace to those who were near.*

EPHESIANS 2:17

Christ is the source of our peace. He made peace with God possible for us: "Therefore, since we have been made right in God's sight by faith, we have peace with God because of what Jesus Christ our Lord has done for us" (Rom. 5:1). The unique relationship of peace between Creator and creature became possible through Christ's sacrificial death.

When it seems as if there is no order in your life, remember that Christ's peace creates order from chaos. Then your peace need not rely on your feelings, emotions or state of mind, but on your relationship with God through Jesus Christ. He is, after all, the source of all genuine and lasting peace.

*Holy Lord Jesus, my salvation and peace are found in
You alone. Let this certainty remain the mainstay
of my peace, calm and undying hope. Amen.*

Light in Times of Darkness

*Even in darkness light dawns for the upright, for
the gracious and compassionate and righteous man.*

PSALM 112:4

Every believer must accept that there will be
times when dark clouds of affliction will cover
your path. At first God is such a glorious reality
to you and joy floods your life, but the clouds
of despondency will soon appear.

When that happens, it is essential to re-
establish the truth that God is unchanging; His
love for you is exactly what it has always been.
You may find the darkness hard to accept and
God may seem far off, but hold on steadfastly
to the assurance that God loves you and that He
cares for you.

Fortunately the dark times do end and you
will step out of the shadows with new strength
and walk in God's sunshine again.

*I will trust You in the darkness, because
I know that You are good. Amen.*

Plan with God

*So that your faith might not rest on
men's wisdom, but on God's power.*

1 CORINTHIANS 2:5

Have you ever experienced the disappointment of seeing carefully planned dreams fall apart? Many people who experience such a setback are unwilling to take any other risks.

Don't let that happen to you – don't let your potential lie wasted and unused. When you trust God in everything you do and submit to His will and obey Him, you might feel that things move too slowly for you, but be patient. Steadfastly put your trust in God and you will find peace of mind knowing that God is in control and that the fulfillment of your plans will be to your lasting benefit.

*Lord, I know that when I bring my plans for my life
to You, You will show me what Your plans are, and
You will help me to succeed in all things. Amen.*

God's Presence

At this, Abram fell face down in the dust.
Then God said to him, "This is My covenant with you."

GENESIS 17:3–4 (NLT)

Abraham didn't respond to God's declaration by saying, "That's fine with me, Lord. From now on we walk together, hand in hand." He knew that he was in the presence of the Almighty, Sovereign God. He fell on his face in reverence for God, acknowledging that God is the Sovereign Authority in the universe.

This response was also an indication that he submitted himself to God and to God's covenant; that he accepted God's will without question. The Almighty God is not something you keep in your pocket and take out when you have no one else to talk to. He is the Creator God, the King of kings. Be humble and respectful and react to His commands with worship and submission.

Heavenly Father, I fall in silence before You.
You are the Almighty Creator, the King of kings.
None can compare with You. Amen.

Your Divine Companion

The righteous cry out, and the Lord hears them;
He delivers them from all their troubles.

PSALM 34:17

Many people struggle with loneliness for a variety of reasons. When you find yourself feeling depressed and lonely, Satan will try to sow seeds of doubt, discouragement and despair in your heart, making you want to give up hope.

But don't give up! The hand of God rests on you always. Rather lay your fears and worries at the feet of the living Christ. Open up your heart and life to the Holy Spirit and He will fan the flame of hope once more, allowing it to burn brightly and light your path.

Powerful Redeemer, grant me the strength to keep my hand firmly in Yours even under the most difficult circumstances. Lead me from the darkness into Your wonderful light. Amen.

Light up Your Life

When Jesus spoke again to the people, He said,
"I am the light of the world. Whoever follows Me will
never walk in darkness, but will have the light of life."

JOHN 8:12

Darkness can cause fear, depression, loneliness and sorrow. The darkness of the soul has a similar effect on people. When light comes, it brings relief and a feeling of safety.

The light of hope and peace flickers and dims when we face afflictions and trials. The only way to overcome the darkness is to turn to Christ. Instead of fearing the darkness, light a small candle of faith to brighten it.

Walk in His light and soon you will find that the darkness has passed. With His light in your heart, each day becomes radiant for you.

*Loving Guide, while You hold my hand I am safe
and secure. Strengthen my faith daily. Amen.*

On the Way with Christ

They asked each other, "Were not our hearts
burning within us while He talked with us on
the road and opened the Scriptures to us?"

LUKE 24:32

Quiet moments spent in the presence of God
are precious. During these moments you draw
inner strength from Him and your spirit is
united with His. Unfortunately, at times when
we are busy, it can easily happen that we
neglect our quiet times.

However, when you have met with God
you will find it easier to concentrate on Him
during those busy times when your thoughts
are in turmoil and storms rage around you.
Use such moments to confirm His presence
and acknowledge His authority in your life.
You will then experience the joy of His closeness and Christ will be your Companion and
Leader every day that you walk life's road.

*Please help me, O Lord, to be aware of Your
presence every moment of the day, and in this
way strengthen the bond between us. Amen.*

God's Sufficient Grace

"My grace is sufficient for you, for My power is made perfect in weakness."

2 CORINTHIANS 12:9

All of us, at one point or another, when faced with a certain situation feel hopeless and defeated.

Yet whatever the predicament you are in, however dark the outlook, never underestimate the extent of God's love for you and the expanse of His grace. Look at examples in the Bible or in history when God transformed despair into hope and defeat into victory through His grace.

He is waiting for you to turn to Him and trust in Him. Your faith will be rewarded and, in His own wonderful way, He will deliver you.

God, through the years You have proved Yourself to be faithful. Therefore I will hold on to Your hand in the future because Your grace is sufficient for me at all times and under all circumstances. Amen.

Love Fills the Heart with Hope

Brothers, we do not want you to grieve like the rest of men, who have no hope.

1 Thessalonians 4:13

Hope and despair are found in the hearts of people and not in circumstances. Love is so important because it causes hope to triumph. When things are at their darkest, hope rises through love to light the darkness of night. There is no room for despair; God has enough love to avert it. He has woven hope into the nature of man so that we can trust in the future.

When all is hopeless, it is hope that keeps us going. Hope strengthens the soul so that we can hold on to eternity and on to the love of God. His love is infinite; He gives us hope out of love.

Lord, may I never believe that anyone is hopelessly lost, because, in love, You sent Your Son to save the lost. Amen.

Walk in the Light

This is the message we have heard from
Him and declare to you: God is light;
in Him there is no darkness at all.

1 JOHN 1:5

Many things that happen in the world today are symptoms of a sick society. The average person feels unable to confront the evil around him or her, which can give rise to an attitude of complete despair.

Nothing in our modern world can be as appalling as the crucifixion on Golgotha. And yet the Light broke through that darkest moment in history, when Jesus overcame the forces of evil and rose triumphantly from the dead.

Regardless of how dark your circumstances may be, put your trust in Christ, follow Him and you will see how His light expels the darkness from your life.

Lord Jesus, in Your light we can see light.
Help us to see Your light in this dark world so
that the darkness will be dispersed. Amen.

Take Heart!

Be strong and take heart, all you who hope in the Lord.

PSALM 31:24

Courage is built on two pillars: faith in your goals and trust in your abilities. God will supply the determination and the strength for both. While we are holding on to God's promises, our courage will grow and become strong. God didn't say that we would never be tempted or suffer trials, but He did promise that He will keep us safe.

The most enriching experience is not found in superficial pleasures, but in our most painful sorrow. If we hold on courageously in faith, sorrow serves a holy purpose in our lives. Romans 8:18 states, "I consider that our present sufferings are not worth comparing with the glory that will be revealed in us." Therefore, take heart!

Loving Father, renew my courage and release me from my fears. Strengthen me to follow in the steps of Christ Jesus, my Savior. Amen.

I Will Always Have Hope

As for me, I will always have hope; I will praise
You more and more. My mouth will tell of Your
righteousness, of Your salvation all day long.

PSALM 71:14–15

What an incredible privilege it is to tell others
of the wonderful things that God has done for
you. Recall God's protection and guidance in
your life and tell someone about how He has
helped you in the past.

Place your trust and hope in God. Believe
that He will never leave you but will strengthen
you and be with you in every time of trial and
affliction. Let the psalmist's praises be your example and may you also have such a passion
to declare the praise of God as long as you live.

*Loving Master, I am overwhelmed at all that
You have done and I want to be a witness to
Your goodness to everyone I meet. Amen.*

Open the Eyes of My Heart

I pray also that the eyes of your heart may be enlightened in order that you may know the hope to which He has called you, the riches of His glorious inheritance in the saints.

EPHESIANS 1:18-19

At the time of writing this, Paul was confined to a prison cell in Rome, under the constant watch of the Roman guard. But who could possibly tell from his prayer that anything was wrong! Paul's faithful description of God's power does not allow even a hint of hopelessness or despair to filter through. Instead he talks of the "glorious inheritance" of a future in heaven.

Paul's eventual hope was not in earthly people, but in heaven, eternity and God. The eyes of his heart could see clearly. Are the eyes of your heart open?

Wonderful Redeemer, help me, through Your Holy Spirit, to grasp the wonderful future that You have made possible for me. Amen.

Praise the Lord,
All You Nations

"Praise the Lord and sing praises to Him, all you peoples."
May the God of hope fill you with all joy and peace as
you trust in Him, so that you may overflow with
hope by the power of the Holy Spirit.

ROMANS 15:11, 13

We praise and honor the birth of David's descendant, our Lord and Savior, Jesus Christ. We place all our hope in Him for our salvation. Pray daily that you will find hope and peace in Him.

"May the God of hope fill you with all joy and peace as you trust in Him, so that you may overflow with hope by the power of the Holy Spirit." What a blessed way for one person to greet another!

Take time out today and thank God for His hope and allow it to spill over into every aspect of your life.

Lord Jesus, may all people on earth experience
Your hope, peace and joy today. Amen.

Trust in God Alone

In Him our hearts rejoice, for we trust in His holy name.
May Your unfailing love rest upon us, O LORD,
even as we put our hope in You.

PSALM 33:21–22

We all need security. When difficult situations threaten to overwhelm us, most of us lean heavily on family and friends for help and support. But this prayer reminds us that, in the long run, only the Almighty God can protect and save us.

It is fitting to admit our dependence on the Lord when we come to Him in prayer. Remember that He is our Shield and Protector. As we focus on this wonderful truth, our fear will turn into praise.

Become quiet for a few minutes and think about the ways in which you seek security, in both big and small situations. Then confess to God that you will trust fully in Him alone.

*Lord Jesus, our hope and salvation surround us with
Your unfathomable love and protection. Amen.*

Praise for the Ways of God

Then my soul will rejoice in the Lord and delight
in His salvation. My whole being will exclaim,
"Who is like You, O Lord?"

PSALM 35:9–10

The splendor of all people fades in comparison with the mighty deeds of God. One day all people will bow before God in worship and declare His might and justice with loud cries. On this day all honor and glory will be given to Him.

But don't wait for that day. In your prayer time today, follow David's example and praise and thank God for saving you and allowing you to put your trust and hope in Him.

*Loving Father, no one can compare with You.
Therefore I will praise You as long as I live. Amen.*

Praise for God's Power

*The seas have lifted up their voice. Mightier than
the thunder of the great waters, mightier than
the breakers of the sea – the LORD on high is mighty.*

PSALM 93:3-4

Through the ages people have marveled at the wonders of God's creation; especially the seas. The angry waves that break against the rocks and crash along the coast demonstrate the overwhelming power of water.

And yet, as powerful as the water is, the might of the God who created everything far surpasses all the powers of nature. Nothing in nature can be compared to the might of God.

If God's power is so much greater than the might of nature, He can undoubtedly handle any human problems. Don't allow desperate situations to undermine your trust in God. When you pray today, remember that God is mightier than the waters of the sea.

*Creator God, we praise and glorify You because
You are mightier than any created force in nature,
and You put Your power at our disposal. Amen.*

august

COMFORT AND COMPASSION

Comfort for the Future

Now the dwelling of God is with men, and He will live with them. They will be His people, and God Himself will be with them and be their God.

REVELATION 21:3

Fear casts a very dark shadow over the future. But when you find refuge in the living Christ, you realize that regardless of how ominous things might appear, everything is still under God's control. The Lord God Almighty still reigns and has not abandoned His Creation.

To believe that God is working out His divine plan, in spite of man's sinfulness, enables you to maintain a well-balanced and calm attitude.

So, you can either look to the future without God and feel depressed and fearful, or you can believe in God's plan of redemption for mankind and approach the future with trust and confidence.

Eternal God, I believe that You are in control of this world. Therefore I can face the future with confidence and hope in Your salvation. Amen.

The Compassionate Christ

*When He saw the crowds, He had compassion
on them, because they were harassed
and helpless, like sheep without a shepherd.*

MATTHEW 9:36

Compassion is one of the outstanding characteristics of the unique personality of Jesus Christ.

The attitude that He revealed when talking to people not only stimulated their minds, but captured their hearts as well. They felt His love for them and responded by loving Him in return.

Because the immortal Christ is still alive, His compassion for humankind is just as real and true today as it was when He walked the dusty roads of Palestine. If you don't know where to turn for strength and inspiration, then remember the compassion of Jesus Christ. He is with you in all your distress and encourages you through the power of His love.

*Savior, may Your love and compassion
inspire and strengthen me today. Amen.*

Compassionate Care

Then they sat on the ground with him for seven days and seven nights. No one said a word to him, because they saw how great his suffering was.

JOB 2:13

Job's friends probably did not know why their friend had to suffer so terribly, there's no doubt about the sincerity of their sympathy. Without saying a word, they just sat with him for seven days and seven nights. Their wordless presence was a balm for Job's distressed spirit.

Stand firm in your faith when facing adversity. Going through hardship will allow your sympathy for others to increase. Then you will become a source of power and faith to the person who is suffering – even if you are unable to express yourself eloquently. Just knowing that you are compassionately and prayerfully present will be a great comfort to the suffering soul.

Strengthen me, dear Lord and Master,
so that I may become a source of power
and comfort to those who suffer. Amen.

God Is a Father Who Cares

There you saw how the LORD your God carried
you, as a father carries his son, all the way
you went until you reached this place.

DEUTERONOMY 1:31

Life is seldom a smooth, problem-free road;
times of peace and calm alternate with frustration, disappointments and setbacks.

If you yield to the temptation of being controlled by these feelings, your life will become
empty and aimless – robbed of its joy, purpose
and meaning.

Nobody escapes the disappointments of life,
but people who have faith in the promises of
God know that He is with them during the
hard times.

When a crisis occurs in your life, the wise
thing to do is to turn to God. Remember you
can, "cast all your anxiety on Him, because He
cares for you" (1 Pet. 5:7).

*God, in times of crisis, I turn to You because
I know You love me and will help me,
no matter what I face. Amen.*

Comfort and Strength

*May our Lord Jesus Christ Himself and God our Father,
who loved us and by His grace gave us eternal
encouragement and good hope, encourage your hearts
and strengthen you in every good deed and word.*

2 THESSALONIANS 2:16–17

When Paul wrote this letter to the church in Thessalonica, he was deeply concerned about the persecution they were bound to face.

Paul never sugar-coated true Christian discipleship. Above all, he wanted Christians to be willing to endure affliction for Christ's sake.

This prayer reveals a fatherly concern, prayed from his heart for the congregation because he could not always be with them. He prayed for God to comfort them and to give them strength. These promises are meant for all God's children. We can draw near to God and ask Him to comfort us and give us strength.

*Lord Jesus, comfort our hearts and give us strength
to do and say only what is right and true. Amen.*

The Blessing of a Broken Heart

*"Blessed are those who mourn,
for they will be comforted."*

MATTHEW 5:4

If you are lost in sadness and sorrow, remember that your Great Comforter and Friend holds your hand firmly in His. You have a Mediator who died on the cross for you, rose from the dead, and ascended to heaven where He interceded for your comfort.

Christ never leaves you in your distress. He is with you in the fiery oven, in the stormy seas, and in the valley of the shadow of death.

Trust in Him who will not allow anything to happen to us that will harm us. God Himself said, "Blessed are those who mourn, for they will be comforted."

Jesus, Man of Sorrows, You drank Your cup of bitterness to the lees. Help me to do the same. Amen.

Comfort through Tears

*Record my lament; list my tears on Your
scroll – are they not in Your record?*

PSALM 56:8

Tears allow us to release our sorrow and grief
in a natural way. They are not a sign of weakness,
but arise from love, tenderness and compassion.
Tears alleviate our sorrow and hasten
the healing of our hearts. God is moved by our
grief and, through our tears, He provides us
with a way of dealing with sorrow.

When Jesus wept, God showed us the sanctity
of tears. He was powerful enough to remove
the cause of sorrow, yet human enough
to shed tears Himself.

Thank God for the healing, delivering and
purifying power of sincere tears. They soften
grief, bring acceptance and lead to joy.

*O Holy Comforter, I thank You that I can find
comfort and solace through my tears; that they make
my grief bearable and bring me closer to You. Amen.*

Share Your Burdens with Christ

Cast all your anxiety on Him because He cares for you.

1 PETER 5:7

There are many aspects of life that can keep us up at night, but it is when we are facing these problems that we must trust God. Jesus promised never to abandon us. He even invites those who are weary and overburdened to come to Him for rest. He will never turn away anyone who comes to Him.

God does not necessarily offer you instant solutions, or make all your problems simply disappear because you pray. But if you place your faith and trust in God and confide in Him in prayer, He will enable you to think clearly and act positively. In His strength you will be able to handle your problems according to the will of God.

Soothe my restless heart, O Holy Spirit. Calm the tempestuous storms that rage. Lead me to quiet waters so that I can experience peace of mind. Amen.

He Carries Us Day by Day

Our God is a God who saves; from the Sovereign
LORD comes escape from death. Surely God
will crush the heads of His enemies.

Psalm 68:20-21

In the presence of God, meditate on the image that's presented in this passage. Place yourself in David's shoes. When you talk to God about your needs and concerns, imagine that God's arms are surrounding you with loving protection and allow His encompassing presence to comfort you.

What images do you have in your mind when you pray? Do you have a picture of a loving Father who hears the cries of His child? Or of a mighty warrior who has charge over countless legions of angels who are ready to do His bidding?

David's prayer provides an intimate image of God who carries His child in His loving arms.

Thank You, Lord, that You carry me to safety in Your eternal arms and that I am always safe with You. Amen.

The Compassionate Jesus

You are a forgiving God, gracious and compassionate,
slow to anger and abounding in love.

NEHEMIAH 9:17

Compassion is a distinctive characteristic of Jesus' personality. It flowed from the very center of His heart and filled His teachings. People enjoyed listening to Him and walked many miles just to hear Him. The brief record that we have of what He did and taught in three years reveals the depth of His wisdom and the uniqueness of His revelation of God the Father.

If life has disappointed you, or if you have failed and are filled with despair and have no idea where to turn to for inspiration and strength, remember the compassion of Jesus. In the power of His love He encourages you to persevere and to rebuild your life.

Compassionate Lord, thank You for
Your love that renews my life. Amen.

Christ Cares for You

"For I am the Lord, your God, who takes hold of your right hand and says to you, Do not fear; I will help you."

ISAIAH 41:13

At times the burdens of life can seem quite overwhelming and all the blessings you've received seem to have vanished. It might sound very courageous to state that you can handle everything that life throws at you, but if your spirit is broken and your ability to recover has diminished, you need a real and vital relationship with God to help you get through.

The glorious truth is that God cares for you. He longs to share your life with you. Every burden and anxiety will be a new opportunity to grow in the presence of God.

Holy Father, I am strengthened and inspired when I consider the great sacrifice of love that You made for me. Amen.

Compassionate and Merciful Is the Lord

The Lord is compassionate and gracious,
slow to anger, abounding in love.

PSALM 103:8

We often pray for our family, loved ones, friends and people in need, but some of our prayers need to be exclusively about God. That is what David did in Psalm 103; he praised the unequivocal love of God.

David praises God because He does not remain angry forever, and He does not punish us as we deserve. His love is as great as the span of the heavens above the earth. He removes our sins from us so that we do not need to dwell on them any longer.

David expresses His gratitude and admiration for God's greatness. Follow David's example and spend the next few minutes expressing gratitude to God in prayer.

Lord, our Lord, You are compassionate and merciful,
long-suffering and full of love. For that we
praise and thank You. Amen.

"Be Still, and Know that I am God"

The LORD said to Job: "Will the one who contends with the Almighty correct Him?" Then Job answered the LORD: "I am unworthy – how can I reply to You?"

JOB 40:1-4

Job lost everything. He was left with a few friends who tried to understand what had happened to him, but they did not recognize God's eternal wisdom.

God does not need to give an explanation to any of us. His knowledge and might far surpass ours. We might never fully understand His ways, but we should know enough of His loving nature to be able to trust Him.

Bring your difficult questions to God, but be careful that they don't become an excuse to blame Him for your problems. God is righteous and His actions and thoughts are far above your understanding.

Righteous God, I do not always understand the things that happen, but I am content in the knowledge that You have all the answers. Amen.

A Prayer in Times of Discouragement

My soul is weary with sorrow; strengthen me according to Your word. Keep me from deceitful ways; be gracious to me through Your law.

PSALM 119:28–29

To whom do you turn when you feel completely disheartened? Turn to the Word of God and His commandments. There you will find renewal. Even the psalmist who was weary and "laid low in the dust" (Ps. 119:25) found renewal in wanting to know more of God and His ways.

In the secular and self-assured world we live in, despair is fairly common. Even when you feel most discouraged, seek God's help to enable you to fully understand this truth: God knows about our discouragement and despair and He will handle every situation that comes our way.

God of Comfort, I weep from sorrow and despair. Encourage me through Your Word. Amen.

The Sound of Silence

After the fire came a gentle whisper.
1 KINGS 19:12

To enjoy and appreciate silence is one of the small joys of life. It is then that your spirit becomes receptive to the presence of God.

Enter the silence with a prayer that the Holy Spirit will fill your thoughts with a Christian quality – it can be any aspect of His holy Being that appeals to you at that moment. When you are alone with God in silence and you become aware of His living presence, your time of quiet reflection becomes a time of spiritual empowerment and inspiration.

In God's presence you can gather strength for daily life with all of its demands and responsibilities.

Lord, I will wait upon You in quiet trust.
I know that You will disperse my doubts
and strengthen my faith anew. Amen.

God Wants to Be Your Partner

Devise your strategy, but it will be thwarted; propose your plan, but it will not stand, for God is with us.

ISAIAH 8:10

Many of us view certain circumstances with trepidation and fear. The only safe way to venture on life's journey with any certainty is to do so in partnership with God. He created the world and everything in it – including you, and He will not allow His Creation to be overpowered.

In order for you to conquer your fears and anxieties amidst threats and adversities, it is essential for you to have an intimate relationship with the living Christ. You must be one in spirit with Him so that, through the Holy Spirit, He can work in and through you. Then you will be able to face every challenge and danger in God's ever-victorious name.

Thank You, Lord, that You clothe me in armor so that I may remain standing in this world. You deliver me from evil and lead me to victory. Amen.

God As Your Guide

Is anyone of you in trouble? He should pray.
Is anyone happy? Let him sing songs of praise.

JAMES 5:13

When you confront a problem in life, you must never forget to go to the One who mercifully offered to be your Father, with your distress, anxiety and confusion.

Find consolation and strength in Jesus Christ because He cares for you and He fully understands your distress and anxiety. Go to the throne of mercy and lay your problems before Him. Give yourself fully to Him in serious prayer and supplication. Then experience the serenity and peace of mind that only He can give you.

Thank God that He lays His hands on you, guiding you safely through the labyrinth of life.

God, You are the only true Comforter. Thank You for
inspiring me and strengthening me time after time.
You are my refuge and my shelter. Amen.

Do God's Work

Never tire of doing what is right.

2 THESSALONIANS 3:13

How often have you met people who feel that there is little or no sense in trying to do the right thing, or to live a life caring about other people?

Regardless of how justified you might feel in adopting this attitude, it will only lead to self-centeredness and a feeling of complacency.

It also clashes directly with the doctrines of Jesus Christ. In spite of the thankless disposition of people, He gave His all to mankind and never gave up on us.

In today's world it is not easy to display the attitude of Jesus. However, you must remember that what you do for other people, you also do for the Master.

Lord, please strengthen us. Give us a steady hand in order to never cease doing Your work. Amen.

You Are Special to God

For God does not show favoritism.

ROMANS 2:11

God has no "favorites". Whether you are an ordinary person, or a celebrity, in God's eyes you are special because you are one of His creatures; His child and He loves you. You are a unique creation of His hand and you have special value in His eyes.

So many people torture themselves with the thought that they are unworthy in comparison to other believers, or that they have disappointed God. But Jesus reached out to both the worthy and the unworthy. They all received His love, care, grace and compassion.

Do not give in to feelings of inferiority or unworthiness. Jesus came for the salvation of all people; both the righteous and sinners.

I know that You live and that You have forgiven my sins. Through Your precious blood I have inherited peace. Amen.

God Is Always with You

For men are not cast off by the Lord forever.
Though He brings grief, He will show compassion.

LAMENTATIONS 3:31–32

There are some people who believe that they are totally alone in this world. They feel that they have no one to turn to for help and comfort in times of trouble.

Although it is true that some people do not enjoy the warmth of a family life, or the company of intimate friends, it does not mean that they are alone. God is always with us. He even says, "Surely I am with you always, to the very end of the age" (Matt. 28:20).

So if you feel all alone, turn to Jesus this very moment and remember that He will never leave you nor forsake you.

You are so patient, Lord. You will never forsake man in his feebleness, but You will always be by our side in compassion. Thank You for Your presence. Amen.

When the Past Haunts You

*One thing I do: Forgetting what is behind
and straining toward what is ahead.*

PHILIPPIANS 3:13

If you are haunted by thoughts about "what could have been", you cannot experience the freedom of spirit that is your spiritual heritage. Perhaps a foolish decision or misguided action robbed your life of peace and joy.

Through the merciful atonement of Christ, you see a vision of what you can become in Him. The past might stir burning shame in your heart, but the shining halo of the future supersedes the dismal gloom of the past.

When you choose a new life in Jesus, you look ahead to a sparkling future, where you start every day anew with God – undisturbed by negative thoughts about failures and flaws of the past.

*We cannot cease praising You for Your miraculous
works of redemption. Through Your mercy,
even Your weakest child is redeemed. Amen.*

With Hope in Our Hearts

O my Comforter in sorrow, my heart is faint within me.

JEREMIAH 8:18

Jeremiah preached his heart out, but the people disregarded and ridiculed the serious messages that he brought them. He was afraid that the coming punishments of God would destroy his country and his people. Sorrowful and dejected, he turned to the only Source of help that he knew: God! He sobbed out, "O my Comforter in sorrow, my heart is faint within me."

In our day of sorrow and pain we can also pour out our sorrow before God. If God is the sunshine of your life when things are going well, He is also your lamp in the darkness of midnight. When your heart is overwhelmed and many difficulties greatly upset you, put your hope in God, your personal Comforter.

Somewhere in the shadows of life we find You,
Lord Jesus. And we recognize You by the
nail marks in Your hands. Amen.

A Caring Heart (1)

"Blessed are the merciful, for they will be shown mercy."
MATTHEW 5:7

Mercy is to personally care about another's distress and to show understanding for the circumstances of others. In the parable Jesus tells in Luke, He describes three types of people: Takers, Hoarders and Givers.

The highwaymen are the Takers. Their philosophy is: "Everything that is yours, is mine. I'll take it." They rob the innocent traveler and walk away from the scene. These people are not necessarily your enemies, sometimes they are even your friends who take everything that they can from you and then leave you to your fate.

Takers are only interested in what they can obtain for their own selfish purposes. They have yet to understand what mercy is all about.

*Lord Jesus, give me a caring heart such as
You had for sinners, prostitutes and outcasts,
so that I can do Your work in this world. Amen.*

A Caring Heart (2)

"Blessed are the merciful, for they will be shown mercy."

MATTHEW 5:7

When a priest and a Levite came along the road and saw a man lying there, they moved to the other side. These are the Hoarders in life whose philosophy is, "Everything that is mine, is mine. I'll keep it." They are people with callous hearts, who gather only for themselves.

Then a Samaritan came upon the wounded man and felt deeply sorry for him. He represents the Givers in life – people who practice mercy and display Christian love. Their philosophy is, "Everything that is mine, is yours. I'll give it." The Samaritan gave of his money, possessions, time, sympathy and comfort without even asking whether it was deserved.

When we show mercy to others, God will have mercy on us.

Lord Jesus, thank You for having mercy on me when I did not deserve it. Help me to do the same for my fellow man. Amen.

A Temple of God

For this God is our God for ever and ever;
He will be our guide even to the end.

PSALM 48:14

This psalm of the Sons of Korah is about the temple and the God of the temple. The God of the temple is more important than the temple itself – this must be true of us as well.

Our religion should point to God, and not to the structures that we erect around our religion. We must worship the Lord in such a way that people notice Him rather than beautiful clothes, expensive buildings and lofty prayers.

Then our lives will have the quality of Jerusalem, the city that points to God and displays the glory of God.

Eternal and unchanging God, thank You that You are also my God and that You will guide me safely into the house of the Father. Amen.

Who Am I?

Yet to all who received Him, to those who believed in His name, He gave the right to become children of God.

JOHN 1:12

In all of our lives there are days when everything looks dismal. In times of dejection and depression, it is not uncommon for people to question their identity and the purpose of life.

If you find yourself doing this, remember the glorious heritage that you have received through the grace of God. Through your faith in Jesus Christ, and by embracing Him as your Savior, your life will find new meaning and purpose because you no longer have to search for your identity. You identify with the living Christ and become a child of God. Life can have no greater meaning than that.

God of grace and love, help me when life is at its lowest ebb to put my hope and faith in You and to cherish the truth in my heart that I am a child of God! Amen.

Be a Comforter

*They approach and come forward; each helps
the other and says to his brother, "Be strong!"*

ISAIAH 41:5-6

Life is not easy, and there are many factors that contribute to a difficult life.

As a Christian, you are not necessarily free from temptations and problems. However, the difference lies in your approach to these things. Don't just join the choir of moans – that will only create more misery and despair.

If you have the Holy Spirit of the living Christ in you, He will prevent you from sinking into the quicksand of a depressed and negative attitude. You will look for solutions to life's problems, and if the answers escape you, you will be content, in childlike faith, to cast your cares upon Christ. After all, God knows everything about everything and He has a glorious future planned for you.

*Lord, help me to remember that You have a wonderful
plan for my life. Let me take comfort in that. Amen.*

Are You Uninvolved?

Then the LORD said to Cain, "Where is your
brother Abel?" "I don't know," he replied.
"Am I my brother's keeper?"

GENESIS 4:9

Much of the evil in the world can be ascribed to
a lack of involvement in the face of the distress
of our fellow man.

Unfortunately there are many people who,
for a variety of reasons, are inclined to follow
the example of the priest and the Levite in the
parable of the Good Samaritan and "pass on
the other side" instead of feeling sorry for the
victim.

Jesus gave us two commandments that He
emphasized as the most important. Love God
with your entire being, and love your neighbor
as yourself. There is no place in the Christian
faith for ignoring your fellow man. Your concern for the well-being of others is a barometer
of your love for God.

Use me, Lord, to serve amongst my fellow man. Amen.

Caring for Others
Could Cure the World

*Each of you should look not only to your own
interests, but also to the interests of others.*

PHILIPPIANS 2:4

Jesus Christ devoted His whole life to caring for others. His love for people was all embracing. This was obvious in His relationship with everyone He came across. Despite the circumstances, or regardless of them, His first thought was always for others – even when He was nailed to the cross.

Jesus commanded His followers to love one another as He loves us. It is unavoidable that this will include self-sacrifice. In our ministry of love to one another, we must show the same compassion and forgiving love that the Master has for us. Only in doing so can the wounds of this world be healed.

*Holy Spirit of God, fill me with the desire and
ability to love my neighbor as You love me. Amen.*

Be Strong!

Say to those with fearful hearts, "Be strong,
do not fear; your God will come."

ISAIAH 35:4

We all experience discouragement at some point in our lives. If you feel that your dreams have been shattered and your efforts have come to nothing, do not allow self-pity to sow the seed of discouragement in your spirit.

There are spiritual reserves from which you can draw that will give you hope and a sense of purpose. Do not rely on your own sources of inspiration, because when these fail you will lose your vision and become discouraged.

God is your constant source of inspiration. Remember, you do not fight alone against negative feelings and emotions. God is on your side and He is waiting to pick you up so that you may proceed with joy and be ultimately triumphant.

I thank You heavenly Father, that through
the power of Your residing Spirit, I can
triumph over discouragement. Amen.

God's Abundant Comfort

"As a mother comforts her child, so will I comfort you."

ISAIAH 66:13

Do you battle with sorrow? In Gethsemane Jesus experienced such anguish that His sweat was like drops of blood falling to the ground (see Luke 22:39-46). Are you mourning the death of a loved one? Jesus cried at the grave of His friend Lazarus (see John 11:35). Do you feel forsaken, even by God? On the cross Jesus wept because He felt like God had forsaken Him (see Matt. 27:46).

In the midst of our adversity, poverty, needs, cares and worries, Someone who understands and cares comes to us and says, "As a mother comforts her child, so will I comfort you." Trust God to lead you from sorrow to joy by His understanding, loving grace.

Thank You, Lord, for the Helper You sent.
What really matters is not what I have lost,
but that You comfort me. Amen.

september

GOD'S LOVING PROTECTION

Divine Protection

They remembered that God was their Rock,
that God most High was their Redeemer.

PSALM 78:35

Many times in the history of the world it seemed as if all was lost and all hope was gone.

Yet God has saved people and nations from devastation in miraculous ways, and has enabled them to overcome dangers and transform defeat into glorious victory.

These cases should serve as a constant reminder of the victorious omnipotence of God in all spheres of life. No circumstances are too small or too big for Him, and no prayer will remain unheard or unanswered. Only in Him will you find deliverance from your distress.

Lord my God, You are a safe fortress to me,
a shield against every calamity that threatens
to overwhelm me. Knowing this, I step with
confidence into the unknown. Amen.

Omnipotent Protector

The Lord is my rock, my fortress and my deliverer;
my God is my rock, in whom I take refuge.

2 SAMUEL 22:2–3

When we are afflicted and needy, the love and omnipotence of God protects us. We can overcome any challenge or problem if we only steadfastly trust in His loving care and grace.

He will command His angels to watch over us and protect us from any danger. We will not be overwhelmed by evil and left powerless. The ability He gives us to choose between what is good and right and what is wrong, will help us to act wisely.

Through the love that is in our hearts, we give and receive love. Then peace and joy fill our minds and hearts, and we are assured that we have an omnipotent Protector.

Father, I bow before You in grateful humility because You have given me Your light and Your wisdom so that I can always do what is right. Amen.

The Presence of God

The angel of the LORD encamps around
those who fear Him, and He delivers them.

PSALM 34:7

Faith in the abiding presence of God is strengthened when you allow Christ to take full control of your life. To ensure that this truth becomes an inextricable part of you, it must become an integral part of your life and mind. If you constantly reaffirm this truth, not only on bright sunny days but also on dark days, it will become part of your nature. You will just know that God is surrounding and enfolding you with His holy presence.

If you turn to Him purposefully in every dark moment, He can and will become a constant reality. If it feels as if He is distant at this moment, then you need to do something about your relationship with Him. Reaffirm His living presence in your life by surrendering and committing yourself to Him anew.

Thank You, my Savior, that I am not controlled by my emotions but that I can hold on to You. Amen.

The Reassuring Love of God

I love the LORD, for He heard my voice;
He heard my cry for mercy.

PSALM 116:1

There comes a time in each of our lives when we urgently need reassurance for peace of mind and to calm our spirit.

Regardless of how self-assured you may be, there will come a time in your life when you will recognize that you have such a need. But what if there is no one to assist you in your crucial time? What are you supposed to do then?

The answer lies in today's Scripture verse. God is always there as a refuge and help in time of need. He is always there when you need Him, He always hears when you call to Him from the depths and you can be assured that He will answer your prayers.

O Lord, my God, I love You with all my heart and know that all things happen for my good because You love me. Amen.

I Am with You!

"When you pass through the waters, I will be with you;
and when you pass through the rivers, they will not
sweep over you. When you walk through the fire, you
will not be burned; the flames will not set you ablaze."

ISAIAH 43:2

It requires great faith and a strong character to be able to work through adversity and disappointment. Many seemingly strong people eventually collapse under their burdens.

The Lord never promised that our lives would be trouble-free just because we choose to serve Him. But He did promise to be there for us at all times, and help us over life's hurdles. Knowing that you don't have to tackle the afflictions of life on your own is a comforting and reassuring thought.

When problems mar your view and place pressure on you, turn to Christ. He is your heavenly Companion. Overcome your problems in the peace of His presence.

Thank You, omnipotent Father, that I can say with confidence that You are with me day by day. Amen.

A Safe Haven

The LORD is my rock and my fortress and my deliverer;
my God, my strength, in whom I will trust;
my shield and the horn of my salvation.

PSALM 18:2 (NKJV)

We all seek shelter at one time or another. It may be in the security of your home, or a shelter against the wind and rain.

Our spiritual and intellectual faculties are also often ravaged by the storms of life. We all need a safe and secure haven where we can find shelter from these storms and be protected from devastating emotional consequences.

Even when it seems as if everything is lost, entrust yourself to the love of Jesus Christ. However dark the road ahead may seem, Christ, in His love, is your shelter and safe haven.

Thank You, my God, that I find shelter in You and that I will be safe now and for all eternity. Amen.

God Is a Refuge

Let all who take refuge in You be glad; let them
ever sing for joy. Spread Your protection over them,
that those who love Your name may rejoice in You.

PSALM 5:11

When we face a crisis, prayer is sadly only used as a last desperate act when all other efforts have failed.

Even though we are encouraged to call on God throughout Scripture, the average person looks for human solutions first, rather than considering God's loving invitation. Over and over He promises His assistance and grace to those who call on Him in their time of need.

Regardless of what the crisis in your life may be, lay your problem before Him in trust and He will transform your crisis into a blessing.

Father, I am experiencing a crisis. Give me Your peace so that I can see things from Your perspective and make the right decisions. Amen.

Your Anchor in Life

There is no one holy like the LORD; there is no
one besides You; there is no Rock like our God.

1 SAMUEL 2:2

When faced with problems, some people turn
to professional counselors for advice, medical
assistance or friends, while others try to fight
their way through the dilemma in their own
strength.

While all these methods can provide some
help, they can't provide assurance that the
problem won't occur again, or that the person
will be able to handle it if it does. The only sure
and lasting solution comes from God.

Never make the mistake of leaving God out
of your life. Other things can help you survive,
but only God can give you abiding peace.

Savior, by putting my life in Your hands
I know that all things work together for
my benefit because You love me. Amen.

A God Who Encourages

May the God who gives endurance and
encouragement give you a spirit of unity
among yourselves as you follow Christ Jesus.

ROMANS 15:5

If you reach a point in life where you feel discouraged and unable to cope, it is good to
spend quality time in the presence of God.
There you will receive the encouragement that
only He can give.

Be still and surrender yourself anew to Him,
and remember that He is God. In the silence of
His divine presence, you can recall all His glorious promises of encouragement. Remember
that in both the storm and the stillness, God is
with you. He does not want you to remain in
the dark valley of despondency; He will give
you the strength to complete the task He has
set before you.

*Holy God, when life is too much for me,
I withdraw into Your presence and there I find
the comfort and the strength that I need. Amen.*

A Refuge in Times of Danger

Every word of God is flawless; He is a
shield to those who take refuge in Him.

PROVERBS 30:5

A seasoned police officer who had never been
shot at during his thirty years of service, still
wore a bulletproof vest every day. One day he
was shot and the bulletproof vest saved his life.
Fortunately, he realized that as long as he was
wearing that uniform, he would be a target and
therefore he was prepared.

In much the same way God protects His
children. Because we belong to Christ, we are
targets for Satan's attacks. That is why an intimate relationship with Christ is crucial.

Christ's protection not only brings us safety,
but also great comfort. The Almighty God of
heaven is willing to rescue those who seek His
will and who obey Him unconditionally.

*Almighty Protector, be my Shield and Rock in
times of sorrow, weakness and doubt. Amen.*

God Keeps His Promises

*The Lord is my helper; I will not
be afraid. What can man do to me?*

HEBREWS 13:6

We have assurance that God will never leave us nor forsake us. God never makes empty promises, and in His omnipotence and grace He keeps His word. He is the God who makes His promises come true even when circumstances seem to prove the opposite.

While Jacob was on the run, he received this promise: "I will watch over you, wherever you go" (Gen. 28:15). How wonderfully God kept that promise! Before David's death, he encouraged his son, Solomon: "Do not be afraid or discouraged, for the Lord God, my God, is with you. He will not fail you or forsake you" (1 Chron. 28:20). And God did just that!

God is righteous and holy; He is gracious and good and He will never forget you. Whatever He promises, He can and will do!

*Loving Father, thank You that I can
depend on Your promises forever. Amen.*

God Hears My Cry

I call to the LORD, who is worthy of praise,
and I am saved from my enemies.

2 SAMUEL 22:4

There is no greater feeling than arriving home safely after a dangerous journey. We like to tell others about our adventures, but we often forget to worship God with prayers of praise for granting us safe passage.

When God delivers us out of desperate situations, we should remember to come quietly before Him for a while and thank Him for what He has done.

How many evils does God protect us from daily? How often have we felt His loving protection over our lives and our loved ones? How can we then forget to thank Him in prayerful worship?

I worship You, Lord my God, because
You have saved me from so much evil. Amen.

From Where Does My Help Come?

*I lift up my eyes to the hills – where does my help come from?
My help comes from the LORD, the Maker of heaven
and earth. He will not let your foot slip – He who
watches over you will not slumber.*

PSALM 121:1–3

The role of security guards is mainly to protect a building from intruders. If guards do not pay attention to their surroundings, then intruders can easily slip in unnoticed.

The Lord never loses concentration while He watches over you. He watches over you constantly to make sure that you do not stumble or fall. Our God never loses focus and will be our protective covering day in and day out.

The one who prays knows that God will protect him because God, who made the heavens and the earth, who neither slumbers nor sleeps, is able to protect His children perfectly at all times.

*I thank You, Almighty God, that You watch over me
day and night and keep me safe from all danger. Amen.*

Trust in the Lord Forever

You will keep in perfect peace him whose mind is
steadfast, because he trusts in You. Trust in the Lord
forever, for the Lord, the Lord, is the Rock eternal.

ISAIAH 26:3–4

We all want to feel safe. In this prayer of praise
from Isaiah, believers declare that their safety
is in the Lord.

In biblical times, safety meant being able
to live in a city with strong walls that would
keep the enemy out. However, walls of stone
can collapse, but our God will be able to protect and guard the righteous forever. Therefore
believers need never fear anyone!

Allow this Scripture passage to encourage
you to focus your thoughts on the Almighty
God. Reaffirm your trust in Him today and experience the peace that this kind of trust can
bring.

*Sovereign God, help me to focus my thoughts on
You and to trust You at all times, because You are
my protector and my eternal Rock. Amen.*

Our Hiding Place

The LORD is a refuge for the oppressed, a stronghold
in times of trouble. Those who know Your
name will trust in You, for You, LORD,
have never forsaken those who seek You.

PSALM 9:9–10

David went through intense suffering in his
life. He was a fugitive from King Saul, the
mightiest man in the land, and on one occasion
even his own son turned against him.

Therefore, when David praised God for being a refuge for people in danger, he was not
talking in abstract terms. Placing his trust in
God was a matter of life and death for him.
And God never let him down.

In times of trial and tribulation, remember
that God always watches over you. He will
never forsake those who call upon Him, nor let
them down.

*Thank You, mighty God, that we can find a safe refuge
in You and that we can hide in You. Thank You that
You never turn away those who come to You. Amen.*

My Help Comes from the Lord

O Lord, how many are my foes! How many rise up against me!
Many are saying of me, "God will not deliver him."
But You are a shield around me. I lie down and sleep;
I wake again, because the Lord sustains me.

PSALM 3:1-3, 5

If enemies are pursuing you and trying to make you doubt the power of God's deliverance by saying, "God will not deliver you," then do what David did – call on God, who is your shield and protection. If you do this, then you will be able to lie down and sleep in peace, because God will watch over you.

There is no need to ever be afraid because God is our protector. He always looks after His children; He will never stop looking after us.

Lord, my loving God, I know that You watch over me because You are my shield and protection. Amen.

Let God's Love Guide You

You have made known to me the path of life;
You will fill me with joy in Your presence,
with eternal pleasures at Your right hand.

PSALM 16:11

For many people life has lost its purpose. Day after day they plod through a monotonous cycle. This is totally unnecessary. The future belongs to God ... and to you! When you put God first in your life, He becomes your inspiration and He will lead you every day as He promised.

Be adamant about getting to know God better through regular Bible study and persevering prayer. Then you will discover that past failures really belong to the past while the future is bright and promising. Live with Christ every day and you will experience a new quality of life. You will receive only the best from Him if you allow Him to guide you in His love.

Dear Lord, thank You that I can abide in You.
Thank You for teaching me how to live
and for giving me Your joy. Amen.

God Is My Refuge

Your word is a lamp to my feet and a light for my path.

PSALM 119:105

In this Scripture verse, the lamp symbolizes the guidance, wisdom and knowledge that we find in the Word. This life is like a dark wilderness through which we must find a way and, just as a lamp helps a traveler in the dark, the Word is a light on our path so we will not stumble.

Pray for light and truth from God's Word so that you can stay on the path of life. Ask God to guide you through the situations that could become stumbling blocks on your spiritual path and commit yourself anew to Him and His Word today.

Thank You, merciful God, that You light up
our dark path with the light of Your Word.
Help us to use Your light each day. Amen.

Let Your Hand Rest on Your People

Revive us, and we will call on Your name.
Restore us, O Lord God Almighty; make Your
face shine upon us, that we may be saved.

PSALM 80:18-19

When you come to the end of your own reserves and find yourself worn out, there is only one place to which you can flee for refuge. God is your only hope for strength.

God created you to fellowship with Him; He wants you to call on His name. You are the branches of His vine and therefore you are completely dependent on the One who planted you – God Himself.

Thank God for the refuge He offers you and for the love that He showers on you. And when you feel that you cannot go any further, ask Him once again to renew your strength for the road that you must follow.

Provider God, let Your holy countenance shine down
on us in love and provide our basic needs. Amen.

Stay Close to the Shepherd

Even when I walk through the darkest valley, I will not be afraid, for You are close beside me. Your rod and Your staff protect and comfort me.

PSALM 23:4 (NLT)

Scripture never tries to hide the dark shadows of life – not even death. This Scripture verse describes how God is always with us, even in the valley of the shadow of death. Therefore we should fear no evil because God is with us.

From time to time we should recall the moments in our lives where God was with us in the valley. Stay close to Him because He will always be with us, through the rest of the year and for the rest of our lives, because He promised to never leave us.

Omnipresent God, even when I walk through the valley of the shadow of death, I will not fear, because I know that You are always close to me. Amen.

Rest in God's Care

Show the wonder of Your great love, You who
save by Your right hand those who take refuge
in You from their foes. Keep me as the apple of
Your eye; hide me in the shadow of Your wings.

PSALM 17:7–8

You are the apple of the Lord's eye. God will protect you because He will answer your cries of distress; he is bending down, compassionate and interested in your prayer.

Believe in your heart that God will use His power to protect you. When you look to God with expectation, you receive the protection you so desperately seek.

Let this Scripture verse remind you that God is willing and able to protect you faithfully. He is the only One who can truly shield and protect you, so lay your cares at His feet.

*I thank You, Almighty God, that You protect me
as the apple of Your eye. Hide me in the
shadow of Your wings. Amen.*

Seek Shelter with God

My eyes are fixed on You, O Sovereign LORD;
in You I take refuge – do not give me over to death.
Keep me from the snares they have laid for me.

PSALM 141:8–9

A newspaper carried a report about a hiker who got lost and walked through a blinding snowstorm for hours without seeing any sign of life. Exhausted, hungry and almost freezing to death, he was ready to give up hope when he spotted a cabin between the trees.

How welcoming the sight of that cabin must have seemed to the hiker – his refuge and safe fortress. It literally saved his life.

Jesus represents that cabin for us – He is our refuge against the dangers surrounding us. Therefore it is comforting to know that when enemies surround us, we can call on God to deliver us. Cast all your cares and concerns onto God, He is your refuge and safe fortress.

Savior and Redeemer, today I look to You for help. Please open Your hand and provide in all my needs. Amen.

Secure in God

*In the beginning You laid the foundations of the earth,
and the heavens are the work of Your hands. They
will perish, but You remain; they will all wear out
like a garment. But You remain the same,
and Your years will never end.*

PSALM 102:25–27

Are you going through a time of great affliction and misery? Allow the words of this Scripture verse to soothe your worried soul and provide a ray of hope in your desperate situation.

Remember, you are a child of God. This God rises above all our problems, as well as above time and space. He is willing and able to keep His children safe and to let them live in His holy presence forever.

Should you find yourself in distress today because of the problems of life, then let God know of your anxieties and thank Him for providing stability in your ever-changing world.

*O God, my refuge and my fortress, thank You for
the security that You bring into my life. Amen.*

Take Refuge in God

I will sing of Your strength, in the morning I will sing
of Your love; for You are my fortress, my refuge in
times of trouble. O my Strength, I sing praise to You;
You, O God, are my fortress, my loving God.

PSALM 59:16–17

Love between people can be a source of great
joy or of great pain – especially if someone's
love is fickle and unpredictable. However, with
God as your Savior, you need never feel that
His love is fickle. In contrast to human love,
God's love is infallible!

Because of this you can count on God to always be your refuge in times of trouble. When
you experience difficult times, find your power, strength and refuge in the infallible love of
God. It will never fail you.

*Holy God, I seek Your shelter in times of
difficulty and affliction. As I turn to You,
let me experience Your infallible love. Amen.*

Jesus Turns Anxiety into Joy

In this you greatly rejoice, though now for a
little while you may have had to suffer grief
in all kinds of trials. These have come so
that your faith may be proved genuine.

1 PETER 1:6–7

There are times in life when everything seems
empty, dismal and dreary. The good news of
the Christian faith is that you are never alone
in sadness, sorrow and suffering.

There is one condition – you must believe
that Christ is your Savior and fully trust in
Him. Then you have the glorious assurance
that you need never struggle with your problems and anxieties alone. He promised to be
with you always.

If you adhere to this simple condition, you
will experience the peace that surpasses all
understanding. It will support you and keep
you on your feet even under the most difficult
circumstances.

How often, O Lord, did You not turn my anxiety into joy!
I will never be able to thank You enough for that! Amen.

When Things Go Wrong

Do not be afraid or discouraged because of this vast army.
For the battle is not yours, but God's.

2 CHRONICLES 20:15

Sometimes you may feel that there is no reason for you to continue fighting the battle. You feel defeated and want to give up.

When these feelings get the better of you, you have probably ignored God. Overwhelmed by the forces against you, you have allowed the influence of evil to affect you negatively. By displaying such an attitude, you have subconsciously acknowledged that these destructive forces have greater control over your life than the omnipotence of your heavenly Father.

Hold on to the timeless truth, to your loyalty to God, and to everything He represents. Choose to join forces with the dynamic power of justice, and then no negative or destructive force can stand against you.

Lord, help me to count my blessings during crises.
You will never abandon me. Even in difficult
times I can count on Your blessings. Amen.

Our Loving Protector

For the eyes of the Lord range throughout the earth to strengthen those whose hearts are fully committed to Him.

2 CHRONICLES 16:9

Let us never think that we have drifted out of the sphere of God's love. We read in His Word that His eyes range throughout the earth in order to help those who put their trust in Him.

The Lord always knows who places their expectations in Him: He shelters them in times of danger, helps them handle temptations and problems, and comforts them in their sorrow.

What a blessed privilege it is to have such a God as our protector. Wherever we find ourselves while living within His will, we can rest assured that His eyes keep a loving watch over us and that He is ready to hear when we call and to help when we need Him.

We praise Your great name, God, because You never forsake those who trust in You. Amen.

Cheerful in the Face of Adversity

All the days of the oppressed are wretched,
but a cheerful heart has a continual feast.

PROVERBS 15:15

One of the most valuable gifts that the Holy Spirit has bestowed upon God's children is the gift of contagious gladness and joy. However, even the Christian's life is subject to tides of ever-changing emotions. The life of our Lord is an excellent example of this as He also experienced the heights and depths of the spirit. It is impossible for a Christian to always smile.

There are times when you would much rather cry. However, when we set our minds on Christ, a peaceful spirit is established and this generates real joy and gladness. You live in the assurance that God is in control even in the most confusing times of your life. This blessed assurance is worth more than a mere smile or passing emotions.

I praise and thank You, Lord my God,
that I can live joyfully and trustingly
because Your Spirit dwells in me. Amen.

God Performs His Wonders through You

The Lord is my light and my salvation – whom
shall I fear? The Lord is the stronghold of
my life – of whom shall I be afraid?

PSALM 27:1

Sometimes worries beyond your control prey on your mind; you may be concerned about your job, or an increase in rent. If you are anxious and worried about a personal matter, you must remember that God is greater than all the circumstances that could befall you.

For a moment you may have allowed fear and uncertainty about the future to obscure your image of God. However, He is forever constant and He desires to share the deepest experience of your life with you. God's omnipotence will sweep away all petty thoughts and all uncertainty will disappear.

*Your works are perfect, Lord, and even
when I drink from the cup of bitterness;
You will never forsake me. Amen.*

God Hears Your Cry

I call on the LORD in my distress,
and He answers me.

PSALM 120:1

It is essential for you to realize that you are never completely alone and that you are not without friends in this harsh world. Jesus, the living Christ, has promised to never leave nor forsake you. He offers you His friendship and all that He asks from you is to be obedient to His commandment of love.

Secure in this knowledge, you have the assurance of His constant presence in your life. He has already heard your call of distress and answered your prayer.

You know our deepest sorrow and hear our sighs. Help us, Lord, never to forget that You alone are our salvation and support. Amen.

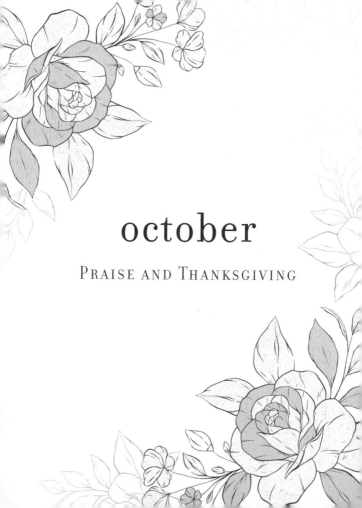

october

PRAISE AND THANKSGIVING

Praise God!

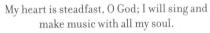

*My heart is steadfast, O God; I will sing and
make music with all my soul.*

PSALM 108:1–2

We pray to thank God for what He has done for us, to lay our needs before Him, and to confess our sins to Him, but we often neglect to praise Him in our prayers.

Never underestimate the power of praise in your life. If someone impresses you, you praise him or her, so why shouldn't you shower God with your praise? He is indeed worthy of our love and thanksgiving.

If you focus on praising and glorifying God, you will create a very special relationship with the living Christ. Your prayer life will be transformed and your love for Him intensified. Through your praise you will become a stronger witness for Him.

*Great and wonderful God, we want to exalt Your name
and glorify You for all the wonders of Your love
and grace that You give to us. Amen.*

True Praise
and Thanksgiving

*Heal me, O Lord, and I will be healed; save me
and I will be saved, for You are the one I praise.*

JEREMIAH 17:14

In Psalm 47 the psalmist appeals to all people to, "Clap your hands, all you nations; shout to God with cries of joy." It is impossible to clap your hands and sing exultantly to the glory of God and still remain gloomy. Praise is a powerful stimulant, so if you are feeling downhearted then start praising and thanking God now.

True praise and thanksgiving to God should not depend on your feelings. It is precisely when you are feeling depressed that you most need to praise Him. When you do, you will experience the wonderful, uplifting power of praise and you will be able to overcome any negative feelings that afflict you.

*I want to lift my heart and my mind to You and exalt
in Your goodness and greatness always. Amen.*

The Blessing of
a Grateful Heart

"He who sacrifices thank offerings honors Me."

PSALM 50:23

Sometimes a complaint is valid, but the danger of complaining is that it can become a bad habit. Eventually you forget that there are more things to be grateful for than to complain about. If you are complaining more often than you are expressing gratitude, then you are living an inferior quality of life.

Never let a day go by without consciously expressing your gratitude. Open your eyes to that which is beautiful around you and praise God for what you see and experience. When you start thanking God for His gifts of grace, He is already planning your next blessing.

Praise the Lord, O my soul, all my
inmost being praise His holy name. Amen.

Giving Thanks

Sing and make music in your heart to the Lord,
always giving thanks to God the Father for
everything, in the name of our Lord Jesus Christ.

EPHESIANS 5:19–20

Many Christians have lost the art of giving thanks. They are so overwhelmed by problems that a cloud of depression has descended upon them and they see very little to thank God for.

When a Christian stops giving thanks, he has lost a source of great inspiration and spiritual strength. Thanksgiving is a powerful force in your spiritual life. It can dispel the dark clouds of depression and despair.

To release the power of thanksgiving, start each day with a sincere prayer of appreciation to God for the gift of life. You will discover that, by doing this, you will establish an atmosphere for the day that will cause you to live in victory.

Holy Lord Jesus, I praise You because of Your great
love for me. Thank You for the gift of abundant
and eternal life that You give to me. Amen.

The Blessing of Gratitude

Give thanks to the Lord, call on His name; make
known among the nations what He has done.

1 CHRONICLES 16:8

In the hustle and bustle of everyday life it is
easy to forget about ordinary courtesy. The
habit of saying "Thank you" enriches every aspect of our lives. Always be ready to express
thanks. You will soon discover how much joy
you can bring to others.

Apart from the fact that you enrich and
bless the lives of others, your own life will be
enriched. Never underestimate the power of
gratitude.

All that we have, our heavenly Father has
given to us. How much more will our lives be
enriched if we learn to express gratitude toward Him?

Grant me a grateful heart, O God, for all the wondrous
things that You have done for us, but above all,
for the birth of Jesus, our Savior. Amen.

Our Wonderful God

To our God and Father be glory for ever and ever.

PHILIPPIANS 4:20

The words "Praise the Lord" are repeated often in the Scriptures. There are many Christians who praise and thank Him daily. Unfortunately, there are also many who take His goodness for granted.

It will be worthwhile to become quiet for a while and consider what your life would have been like without God's love and faithful care. What would have happened if you had lost your job and were left without an income? How would you have felt if nobody loved or cared for you?

As a Christian, you know that you don't have to worry because your heavenly Father knows exactly what you need. He loves you and will take care of you. Praise Him for it.

Praise the Lord, O my soul; all my inmost being, praise His holy name. Praise the Lord, O my soul, and forget not all His benefits (see Ps. 103:1-2). Amen.

Rejoice in the Lord!

Then the people of Israel – the priests,
the Levites and the rest of the exiles – celebrated
the dedication of the house of God with joy.

EZRA 6:16

Many Christians see Christianity as somber and attend church simply out of a false sense of duty. Such an attitude tragically deprives them of the greatest of all joys: joy in the Lord.

God offers you fullness of life. Turn to Him and you will become more aware of His life-giving Spirit. As you open yourself up to the Holy Spirit, you will find that your worship, Bible study and prayer life gain new meaning. If you place your trust in the living Christ, you will discover that God is no longer a remote being, but an integral part of your life.

Worship ought to be a joyful experience. Open yourself to the Holy Spirit and He will raise you from despondency to ecstasy in Christ.

*O Holy Spirit, come into my life and fill
me with the joy of the Lord. Amen.*

Be Continually Grateful

*Continue to live in Him, rooted and built up
in Him, strengthened in the faith as you were
taught, and overflowing with thankfulness.*

COLOSSIANS 2:6–7

Many people tend to focus so much on the flaws around them that they fail to see the wonders of God and His grace.

God knows every detail of your life, from the cradle to the grave. In His eternal design He plans what is best for you. Sometimes things go wrong, but God can change your situation so that light radiates from the darkness, and hope is born from despair.

If you feel dejected, think back on all the good things that have happened in your life. Thank the Lord for His blessings and He will bring healing and joy to your life because God is the Giver of all that is good.

*We praise and thank You, O Lord, with our hearts,
our mouths and our hands, for all the
wonders that You have done. Amen.*

Start Your Day by Giving Thanks

I will give thanks to the Lord because of His
righteousness and will sing praise to
the name of the Lord Most High.

PSALM 7:17

A healthy approach and a positive attitude towards life do not come easily to the average person. We are subject to the whims of our emotions. But it is important that we, as children of God, maintain an optimistic attitude toward life.

When you wake up in the morning, your first responsibility is to take positive control of your thoughts and to thank God for the privilege of a new day and for all His blessings.

It requires an act of will to start every day with true thanksgiving, but the benefits are worthwhile.

*I want to start my day by thanking You for all the
things I so often take for granted – for friends,
family, my health and this new day. Amen.*

Learn to Praise God

You have made known to me the path of life,
You will fill me with joy in Your presence,
with eternal pleasures at Your right hand.

PSALM 16:11

Praise leads you into the throne room of God. When you become conscious of being in His holy presence, you experience exceeding joy and glory like nowhere else on earth!

Praise uplifts you, despite your shortcomings, and creates a totally new relationship between you and God. While you praise and worship Him, you identify with Him through Jesus Christ. It strengthens your faith, joy, zeal and interest in life.

Learn to praise God – and start living on victorious ground. "Praise the Lord. Give thanks to the Lord, for He is good; His love endures forever" (Ps. 106:1).

O God who answers prayers, teach me to
appreciate the power and real value of
praising and worshiping You. Amen.

Offering Praise

He has sent Me to proclaim the year of the LORD's favor
and the day of vengeance of our God, to comfort all
who mourn. They will be called oaks of righteousness,
a planting of the LORD for the display of His splendor.

ISAIAH 61:1–3

Praise and thanksgiving have the power to change lives. When the storm clouds of life obscure the sunshine of God's love; when doubt threatens to destroy our faith in the goodness of God; when life seems to be falling apart – then, more than ever, it is necessary to offer praise and thanksgiving from the depths of our hearts.

You might ask how you can thank and praise God if it seems that there is nothing to thank Him for. Thank God that He is greater than any problem you are facing. As you focus on His greatness, your life will rise above all destructive influences.

O Lord, teach me to rejoice in spite of all the things
that happen. Help me to remember that all things work
together for my good because I love You. Amen.

Think and Thank!

I thank my God every time I remember you.

PHILIPPIANS 1:3

When the path of life becomes steep, and dark clouds threaten to block out all inspiration, pause a while and consider how God has brought you along thus far. Remember all His abundant blessings. At times disaster loomed and you might have felt that everything was lost, but God helped you rise from the ashes of failure.

The key that unlocks the door to a creative life is gratitude. With everything in life, look for something to be grateful for. When you assimilate this truth into your heart, you will approach the future with God-given confidence and the assurance that, in the name of Christ and in His strength, you can triumph over every situation.

Beloved Lord, I recall the blessings of the past and the joys of the present. Thank You for showers of blessings that You pour upon me. Amen.

Gratitude Glorifies God

I will praise You, O Lord, with all my
heart; I will tell of all Your wonders.

PSALM 9:1

Even though religion is a serious matter, some of God's most dedicated servants have been lively, happy people. A faith that is void of humor can hardly express the spirit and attitude of Jesus Christ.

One of the most beautiful things we read about Jesus is that ordinary people enjoyed listening to Him and children were at ease in His presence. This would not have been true had He been constantly gloomy. He emanated a deep peace and happiness – joy and quiet humor enabled Him to love and appreciate people.

Your sense of humor, enriched by your gratitude and love, is a gift from God.

I am so grateful for the way in which Jesus
revealed You to us, Father. Thank You for being
approachable and for Your great love. Amen.

Keep Your Worship Fresh

Sing to the LORD a new song,
His praise from the ends of the earth.

ISAIAH 42:10

It is very easy to fall into a rut when worshiping. Worship in your church might be conducted rigidly without any variation whatsoever; your personal devotions may follow the same pattern day after day.

Your times of worship should be vibrant and exciting. If this is not the case, you should seriously examine your pattern of worship and prayer.

Never be hesitant to vary the form or type of your worship. Change will bring a deeper dimension to your praise and worship. Just make sure that Jesus Christ remains the center of your worship.

Glorified Lord, I want to sing You a new song!
Lead me through the Holy Spirit to worship
You in spirit and in truth. Amen.

Your Personal Worship

Come, let us bow down in worship,
let us kneel before the Lord our Maker.

PSALM 95:6

Worship can entail the interaction of conflicting emotions. Sometimes you will be filled with a sense of awe that causes an irrepressible feeling of spontaneous praise. At other times you lack the inspiration that sparks off worship.

While attempting to understand the eternal God through the life, words and works of Jesus Christ, your worship necessarily becomes more intimate.

To see God through the eyes of Jesus Christ will enable you to worship Him more intimately and affectionately. Wonder, adoration, love and affection are experienced simultaneously when worship is offered in spirit and in truth.

Holy, holy, holy are You, Lord God of hosts.
Draw me forever closer to You in worship. Amen.

Be Thankful in Everything

Better a little with the fear of the
Lord than great wealth with turmoil.

PROVERBS 15:16

The average Christian is so busy looking for a spectacular revelation of the miracle-working God that he is not able to see God at work in the common, everyday things.

When you have learned to appreciate the small blessings from God, you will see how God is at work in your life. The wonder of friendship, the kindness of strangers, and an understanding heart are all expressions of the greatness and the blessings of God.

Make a decision today to never again take anything for granted. Thank God for His blessings and you will unlock the treasure room of God and fill your life with new beauty and riches.

I praise and thank You, gracious Lord, for the small things that make each day so delightful. Help me never again to take daily blessings for granted. Amen.

Serve God with Gladness!

Worship the LORD with gladness;
come before Him with joyful songs.

PSALM 100:2

I praise and thank You, Father, because You created me and then made me a new creation in Christ. Thank You for the beauty of Creation through which You speak to me and where I can draw close to You in worship.

With gratitude I praise You for Your Word, through which the Holy Spirit reveals Your divine will for my life.

I praise and thank You for abundant blessings – for my family, my friends and all the things that make my life worthwhile. Give me a grateful heart always Lord, so that my life may be a song of thanksgiving to Your glory.

I want to sing to the glory of the Lord as long as I live.
You have done great things and
You are worthy of all praise. Amen.

God Is Great

You are my God, and I will praise You;
You are my God, I will exalt You.

PSALM 118:28

God is in control of everything and only He can provide for you, protect and guide you. If you put your trust completely in Him, He will use even your negative experiences to your benefit.

The greatest example of this in Scripture is how He used the awfulness of the crucifixion to establish the glory of the resurrection. There by victory was achieved over sin and death for all time when His love triumphed over evil.

Never cease to praise and thank God, even under appalling circumstances. You can always count on the wonder of His love. He will care for you and never leave you or forsake you. We worship a mighty God who deserves all our praise and thanksgiving.

O heavenly Father, I thank You for all the good
You have done in my life, but also for bitterness and
sorrow; by that You always draw me to You. Amen.

Joyous Christianity

*"My soul glorifies the Lord and my spirit
rejoices in God my Savior."*

LUKE 1:46-47

Some people think that the Christian faith is a heavy, and sometimes unbearable burden. They frown upon any appearance of light-heartedness in spiritual matters. But God intended something far different.

Christianity does not eliminate joy and happiness from life. On the contrary, it fills your life with abundant joy. Through fellowship with Christ you can know the blessing of His presence every day. The more you praise and thank Him, the more happiness you get from life.

Joy is a fruit of the Holy Spirit. Your faith and surrender to Christ should bring His joy to every area of your life.

*Dear Lord Jesus, I continually delight in the
knowledge that You are always with me. Amen.*

The Secret of a Festive Life

*Let us come before Him with thanksgiving
and extol Him with music and song.*

PSALM 95:2

If Jesus Christ abides in you through faith, you develop a keener appreciation of the beauty and depth hidden in the lives of others, as well as in the world around you. The greater your gratitude, the more life will reveal its hidden treasures to you.

It is important to be thankful. All through Scripture we hear the resounding echo of the praise of those who loved God and were grateful for His blessings. We appreciate the blessings, but we love God because He is our Father. Our hearts overflow with gratitude for all He does for us.

*Thank You, Lord Jesus, for all Your love and
gifts that You have granted me. Amen.*

I Will Sing to the Lord

I will sing to the LORD all my life;
I will sing praise to my God as long as I live.

PSALM 104:33

There are many different ways to express your-self in prayer to God when you use Scripture. Allow the Scripture verses to stimulate your prayer life and draw you closer to God. Make them part of your meditations and discover the power of the Almighty God who is able to do all things – the glance of His eye can cause the earth to tremble and set the mountains on fire.

Thus, no matter what enemy confronts you, no matter what mountains block your path, you can be assured that nothing is impossible for our heavenly Father. Therefore, you can leave your enemies, burdens and worries in His hands. He will take care of them for you in His mighty power.

Holy God, I delight in Your power and I want
to praise and honor You in this song. Amen.

All the Earth
Bows Down to You

*How awesome are Your deeds! So great is
Your power that Your enemies cringe before
You. All the earth bows down to You.*

PSALM 66:3-4

The believer need not have any doubt that God answers prayer! And when He does, we should sing His praises and thank Him for His faithfulness.

Today's psalm was written after Israel had won a war under difficult circumstances. The Israelites wanted to testify to each other, to the world, and to God Himself, how great and mighty He is – so that everyone would bow before Him.

To be on God's side is the greatest privilege on earth. Let us thank God with our whole heart because we know He hears our prayers and will always cause us to triumph over our enemies!

*We bow in thankfulness before You God. Thank You
for everything You have done for us! Amen.*

You Give Us Reason to Praise!

We are filled with the good things of Your house, of Your holy temple. You answer us with awesome deeds of righteousness, O God our Savior, the hope of all the ends of the earth and of the farthest seas, who formed the mountains by Your power.

PSALM 65:4–6

God is faithful and eager to answer our prayers and forgive our sins. We need to learn to praise Him with the same enthusiasm we have when we ask for His help. We must also keep the promises we make to God and turn them into deeds of thankfulness.

God is worthy to receive our praise because He answers our prayers and forgives our sins.

Make spending time with God in prayer your greatest joy and tell God how much pleasure it gives you. Burst forth into songs of praise to God and glorify Him today.

Heavenly Father, I will continually sing Your praises because You always fulfill Your promises. Amen.

Spiritual Blessings

Praise be to the God and Father of our Lord Jesus
Christ, who has blessed us in the heavenly realms
with every spiritual blessing in Christ. For He
chose us in Him before the creation of the
world to be holy and blameless in His sight.

EPHESIANS 1:3–4

We should regularly praise and thank God for all the spiritual blessings that He gives to us, such as our salvation and our inheritance in heaven.

Praise Him also for the spiritual blessings that you cannot see, such as joy, inner happiness and hope in your heart. Give praise and worship to our merciful God from whom all our spiritual blessings come.

When the pressures and troubles of life are weighing down on you, praise God for the rich abundance of His blessings that He gives you daily.

Merciful and loving Lord, I praise Your holy name
for all the spiritual blessings in my life. Amen.

I Will Proclaim
Your Great Deeds

One generation will commend Your works to another;
they will tell of Your mighty acts. They will speak
of the glorious splendor of Your majesty.

PSALM 145:4–5

God has many traits that make Him worthy
of our praise and worship; His majesty; His
glory; His mighty acts; His greatness; His
goodness and His righteousness; His loving-
kindness; His faithful love and His grace and
compassion.

For these reasons and many more, we
should be full of praise for God. We should tell
every generation of God's mighty deeds.

Take a few minutes to consider the glory of
God and allow the words of David to lead you
in your own song of praise to the Almighty.
Then make a point of telling someone else
about the wonderful things that God has done
for you.

Holy God, You are surrounded by majestic glory!
Help me to tell others of Your love and grace. Amen.

My Lips Will Shout for Joy

I will praise You with the harp for Your faithfulness,
O my God; I will sing praise to You with the lyre,
O Holy One of Israel. My lips will shout for
joy when I sing praise to You.

PSALM 71:22–23

The writer of these Scripture verses describes himself as old, saying that his strength has failed. But after he had examined his life thoughtfully and prayerfully, this "old" person was bubbling over with joy. He sings the praises of God and brings to remembrance everything that God has done for him.

Far too often we find ourselves praying hesitant prayers to God and our songs of praise are rather half-hearted. Offer up enthusiastic praise to God and feel the joy of the Lord that will stir inside you.

Lord, my God and Father, I will praise You with thanksgiving and singing and tell others of Your wonderful deeds. Amen.

Pay Tribute to
the Awesome God

*You are resplendent with light, more majestic
than mountains rich with game. You alone are to be
feared. Who can stand before You when You are angry?*

PSALM 76:4, 7

Anyone who spends time in the mountains develops an admiration for the power of nature. We often feel small and insignificant against the massive rock formations. God created these gigantic structures to confirm His power.

If the whole of Creation trembles before God's awesome power, how much more should we approach Him in prayer with admiration and holy fear! Praise God for His breathtaking power and might. Surrender yourself and your possessions to Him afresh today; give God the honor and the glory He deserves and bring your offerings of time and possessions to Him today.

*Awesome Father, in Your glory You are mightier
than the majestic mountains. I dedicate myself
and all that I have anew to You today. Amen.*

Thankfulness
Because Our God Reigns

The twenty-four elders, who were seated on their thrones before God, fell on their faces and worshiped God, saying: "We give thanks to You, Lord God Almighty, the One who is and who was, because You have taken Your great power and have begun to reign."

REVELATION 11:16–17

When evil and wickedness go unpunished, we tend to despair of ever finding justice.

The twenty-four elders who sit in the throne room of God praise the Almighty, they thank the One who is and who was because He controls all the events of Earth's history. They praise Him because the earth ensures that justice is served at the right time and in the right place. Do not doubt, because God's justice will triumph.

In your prayer time today, picture yourself in the throne room of God at the end of the ages, what praise and prayer of thanksgiving will you personally offer to God?

Sovereign God, I thank You that You will ensure righteousness to triumph. Amen.

The Lamb Is Worthy to Receive Our Praise

Then I looked and heard the voice of many angels.
In a loud voice they sang: "Worthy is the Lamb!"

REVELATION 5:11–12

The Bible encourages Christians to offer prayers of praise and thanksgiving, which reveal their commitment to God.

Yes, our private devotions are very important, but there is an element missing unless we join together with other believers to praise God. We are fulfilling our calling as worshipers when we, God's children, are caught up in worshiping Him.

It is, after all, from worshipers of every place and age that Christ will receive the worship He so richly deserves. May God help us to always be found in the company of praying people.

Lord Jesus, blessing and honor, glory and power,
belong to You. I pray for the company of other believers
so that we can praise Your name together. Amen.

Praise to My Savior

I will praise You, O Lord my God, with all my heart;
I will glorify Your name forever. For great is
Your love toward me; You have delivered me
from the depths of the grave.

PSALM 86:12–13

When we realize the greatness of what God has done for us, we look for ways to express our love for Him. He has been so good and faithful to us. We should remind ourselves when we pray what a magnificent privilege it is to be able to draw close to God in prayer.

We were in the deep mire of sin, but God raised us up so that we could stand in His holy presence. Do not just take this mercy for granted. Today, ask the Lord to teach you to serve Him with your whole heart so that your life will be a song of praise to Him.

Father, I praise and worship You because You saved me. Help me to walk in Your ways forever. Amen.

Why Should We Praise and Glorify God?

Praise, O servants of the LORD, praise the name
of the LORD. Let the name of the LORD be praised,
both now and forevermore.

PSALM 113:1-2

Why should God be praised and glorified? Why
should we tell Him how mighty and wonderful
He is? Because He asks us to.

God will never ask us to do anything meaningless or ritualistic. The complexity of the human mind compels it to reach out to something
higher and greater than itself. This yearning
can be fulfilled by praising and glorifying God.
Praise connects us to the One who knows and
understands the desires of our hearts.

True praise is one of the greatest inspira-
tional forces in life. It raises you up from your
spiritual despondency and brings you into the
holy presence of God.

*Holy Father, I enter Your gates with adulation, with
praise I go into Your temple court. I enter into Your
presence with joy and thanksgiving. Amen.*

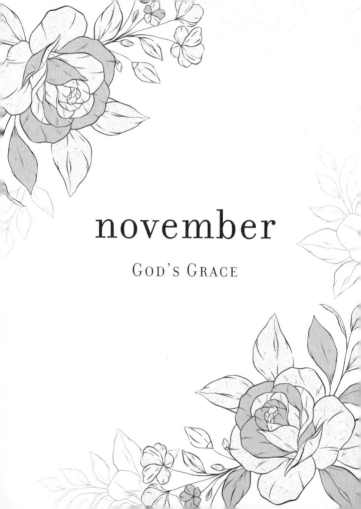

november

GOD'S GRACE

The Grace of a New Beginning

*He who was seated on the throne said,
"I am making everything new!"*

REVELATION 21:5

It is a sign of God's immeasurable grace that no person will ever reach a stage in life where one cannot start over. Each day that dawns is a new beginning. Our God is the God of second chances.

Do not allow whatever may have happened in the past to cause you to lose sight of what the future may hold. If you wish to make a fresh start, make a firm decision to be done with your old life, even though it will still try to enslave you. All new life comes from God alone. Continually affirm that new life flows through you as a result of God's grace, and you will receive the inheritance of new life that is yours in Christ.

*Lord of new beginnings, thank You that each new day
Your mercies are new and I can begin again. Amen.*

Eternal Life

For this very reason, Christ died and returned
to life so that He might be the Lord of
both the dead and the living.

ROMANS 14:9

Many people brood over the unknown. In their uncertainty they fall prey to anxiety and tension.

For the Christian believer there is a glorious truth that emanates from the life, death, and resurrection of Jesus Christ. We know that He is with us right now, leading us through life. He also went to prepare a place for us in God's heavenly kingdom. In this way He assures us that when our earthly life is over, we will be with the Lord forever.

Instead of being consumed with fear and worry, hold on to the promises of Jesus and rejoice in the fact that because Jesus lives, you too will live forever.

Risen Savior, through faith I know that You live and that I too will live eternally with You. Amen.

God Works in Everyday Things

In his heart a man plans his course,
but the Lord determines his steps.

PROVERBS 16:9

God often works in miraculous ways. We see His glory in the changing heavens; we see His handiwork in the grandeur of Creation.

Yet, God is also the Creator of the small and everyday things: the perfection of the rose and the fragility of the forget-me-not. All these reflect a creative God who is also the Master of order and detail.

We so easily forget that God is interested in our well-being. Just consider how many times He has guided you through difficult circumstances.

Thank You, Almighty God, that You never
cease to work in my life and answer my prayers.
You speak with a thousand tongues;
let me always hear Your voice. Amen.

You Are a Child
of Royal Blood

*You are all sons of God through faith in
Christ Jesus, for all of you who were baptized
into Christ have clothed yourselves with Christ.*

GALATIANS 3:26–27

You never need to feel spiritually inferior – especially in comparison to other believers. Remember that when God accepted you as His child, He did not do so on the basis of your knowledge, work or worthiness. In His grace He accepted you based entirely on your faith in Jesus Christ and your acceptance of Him as your Redeemer and Savior.

Jesus accepts you for who and what you are. All He asks is that you believe in Him and accept Him as the Lord of your life. Joyfully respond to this invitation and experience the grace and love of your divine Father every day.

*Holy God, my heavenly Father, thank You that I can,
through faith, claim the privilege of being
called Your child. Amen.*

Know the Grace of God and Live!

Grace and peace be yours in abundance.

1 PETER 1:2

People are always searching for peace to help them deal with their problems. Do not be tempted to seek man-made solutions, as there is only one true method of handling your life with confidence and assurance – and that is in the power of Jesus Christ.

If you commit yourself and your life to Him unconditionally, then you can rest assured that He will give you the grace required to handle every problem. You will thus be blessed with tranquility and peace far beyond human understanding.

Grace and peace become a reality in your life only through God, so don't drift from Him and forfeit what only He can give.

Loving Master, I thank You, because through Your grace You enable me to face and handle every problem that comes my way. Amen.

Indescribable Grace

"I am the vine; you are the branches. If a man
remains in Me and I in him, he will bear
much fruit; apart from Me you can do nothing."

JOHN 15:5

When you find yourself in a situation that makes you feel incompetent and inadequate, do not focus on your own abilities. Jesus made it very clear that we are capable of doing nothing without Him, but that with Him we can do anything that needs to be done.

In this truth lies the answer to all your fears, doubts and insecurities. Whatever you do in life, first take it to God in prayer, seek His help and lay all your expectations, fears and concerns before Him.

By allowing Him to work through you, you will achieve the kind of success that would otherwise be unattainable in your own strength.

Loving Father, I praise You and thank You for the wonderful assurance that I can do all things through Christ who gives me strength. Amen.

God's Grace Is Sufficient

The days of the blameless are known to the LORD,
and their inheritance will endure forever.

PSALM 37:18

We often hear of people who apparently live virtuous lives and yet are plagued by disaster.

Sometimes we want to question God's actions, and it is difficult to agree with Paul when he says, "We know that in all things God works for the good of those who love Him, who have been called according to His purpose" (Rom. 8:28).

However, it is important to remember that God's perspective on life is eternal and He truly desires all things to work for your own good. Paul also says that our present suffering does not outweigh the glory that will be revealed in us (see Rom. 8:18). Take courage and let your heart be peaceful – God's grace is sufficient!

I thank You, all-knowing God, that Your grace is always sufficient for me, despite my problems. Amen.

God's Grace and Your Problems

*In all your ways acknowledge Him,
and He will make your paths straight.*

PROVERBS 3:6

Life can suddenly become filled with problems of all kinds. Regardless of their source, they dominate your life until you find a solution.

If you are experiencing a problem and sincerely seek a solution, direct your thoughts to God and don't focus on the problem. You cannot find a solution to your problem if you do not allow God to assist you.

Allow Him to create order from chaos and to give you the right solution. When God becomes more important than your problem, you will be fueled by a spiritual power because God is occupying His rightful place in your life. You will find solutions to your problems and by His grace you will be able to live victoriously.

Eternal God, I put You first in my life, knowing that You are powerful enough to handle every crisis in my life. Amen.

Being Weak Is Not a Shame

*God chose the foolish things of
the world to shame the wise.*

1 CORINTHIANS 1:27

Never despise yourself because you think you
are weak. The only shameful thing is when you
stop trying to overcome it.

You have the opportunity to develop power
and strength through the grace of the Almighty
God. This power will enable and strengthen
you to become the person God intended you
to be.

Eventually every weakness can be overcome when you become aware of the fact that
God's Spirit can dwell and work in your spirit.
Through the Spirit of grace, you discover that
you have God-given talents and strength which
give purpose and inspiration to your daily existence.

*O Holy Spirit of God, dwell in me so that
I can overcome my weaknesses and become
strong by the grace of God. Amen.*

Chosen by God

"You did not choose Me, but I chose you."

JOHN 15:16

For many people the conscious beginning of their Christianity dates back to when they acknowledged the sovereignty of Christ in their lives. In reality their Christian experience only started when the Holy Spirit started working in their imperfect lives.

You were chosen by God to serve Him and to live to the honor and glory of His name. It may not sound very exciting to you and initially it may not really satisfy you. Those people, however, who submitted themselves unconditionally to the Lord when they heard Him calling, discovered that their lives gained new meaning and purpose.

To be chosen by God for His service: what greater measure of grace could be shown to an insignificant human being?

Lord and Master, You called me by grace to serve in Your mighty kingdom. Grant me the strength and wisdom to live to Your glory and not my own. Amen.

Glory in His Grace

The grace of the Lord Jesus be with God's people. Amen.

REVELATION 22:21

The last words of the Bible are this wonderful benediction. How these words soothe our storm-tossed hearts!

We all, at one time or another, suffer from anxiety – either because of a current situation or because we fear the future. In our human weakness and short-sightedness we are not sure how to act. Some people try to handle everything in their own strength, while others throw their hands up in despair.

Remember, the only way out of a problem, and the only reason for success, is the compassionate love and grace of our heavenly Father. The saving grace of God permeates our lives. Because He loves you, He blesses you with His grace.

O Lord, I thank You for Your grace.
You saved me and redeemed me from death.
You are my heart's desire. Amen.

Grace — Rich and Free!

The grace of our Lord Jesus Christ be with you all.

2 THESSALONIANS 3:18

Where would we be if it were not for the grace of God? The wonderful hymn *Amazing Grace* tells of a prodigal son who came back to the Father's house. John Newton, the writer of the song, says that he was spiritually blind and lost, but the grace of God touched and healed him. This song reminds us of a redeeming God whose love is so great that He gave us His all through grace.

The Son of God took your guilt and my guilt upon Himself and sacrificed His life to redeem us from sin. His grace extends so far that even when we turn away from Him, Christ waits patiently and lovingly for us to turn back to Him.

Thank You, God, that Your grace has set me free and given me new hope for tomorrow. Amen.

Sufficient Grace

You then, my son, be strong in the grace that is in Christ Jesus.

2 TIMOTHY 2:1

Many people are not able to work through the problems they face and fear has a devastating effect on them.

Jesus invites those who are tired and heavy-laden to bring their problems to Him and find rest for their souls. He invites you to bring your anxieties to Him because He cares for you. Turn to God in Christ and He will enable you to handle your problems with courage.

Receive your strength and confidence from Him because in all circumstances His grace will be sufficient for you so that you can deal with your problems in a new, assured manner.

Father, I ask for Your strength to assist me in times of weakness, help me to know Your grace that is sufficient for me. Amen.

To Grow in Grace

"You must be born again."

JOHN 3:7

When a searching soul yearns for God, He will meet that person regardless of where he may be. The important fact here is that you are re-born spiritually and that you know Christ as your Savior.

You need to grow in knowledge and in grace in your spiritual life. While you grow in the spirit and attitude of Christ, you can perhaps look back to a time and place when this wonderful new life started. However, you must never try to stay at that place and time.

Growing spiritually is equally important to experiencing a new spiritual birth. May both be your rich inheritance through the overflowing grace of God.

Lord, my God, I want to grow in knowledge
and in grace so that I can forevermore
draw closer and closer to You. Amen.

Feelings of Guilt

I write to you, dear children,
because your sins have been forgiven.

1 JOHN 2:12

Many people lead negative, miserable lives because they allow feelings of guilt to oppress and wear them down until they break.

Scripture tells us that we are all sinners and that Jesus came to save us. It was an act of grace that culminated in His crucifixion on Golgotha where the Son of God sacrificed His life so that we could be forgiven and redeemed from sin.

Liberate yourself from the chains of guilt and self-condemnation. Turn to Christ in heartfelt remorse and true confession. Accept His redeeming love and grace with a grateful heart. That will enable you to live life to the full as a liberated person.

Thank You, Lord and Savior, that I can live life to
the full, knowing that You have forgiven my sins
and enable me to live according to Your will. Amen.

The Coming Grace

Concerning this salvation, the prophets,
who spoke of the grace that was to come to you,
searched intently and with the greatest care.

1 PETER 1:10

As believers we sometimes sense that God allows certain things to happen; that He has planned wonderful circumstances and has stretched out His holy hand to make sure that everything works out well for us.

The grace of God pours out of the loving heart of the Lord and changes people's lives wherever it goes. It is also destined for you. It will transform you, empower you, build you up spiritually and give you a purpose in life. It will not remove all hardships from your life, but it will give you more resources to help you cope. It is destined for you. Have you received it?

We praise and thank You, Lord Jesus,
for those who have received Your grace
and shared it with others. Amen.

Praise Be to the Lord

Sing to God, sing praise to His name, extol
Him who rides on the clouds – His name
is the LORD – and rejoice before Him.

PSALM 68:4

When we pray for God's grace we should never forget to sing His praises as well. He is our only hope, our strength and our shield. Even while we are waiting for Him to deliver us from our present dilemmas, we can praise Him for His faithfulness to us in the past. Then our faith and trust in the mercy of God will be strengthened.

God is merciful! How often have we been on the verge of giving up in despair because our situation seemed completely hopeless, and then God stepped in and acted on our behalf?

The might of God works in our favor when we call on Him in faith, and then we can give thanks to Him in song.

I praise You, Lord, because You
heard my cry for mercy. Amen.

Our Hope Is in You

Do any of the worthless idols of the nations bring rain?
Do the skies themselves send down showers? No, it is You,
O Lord our God. Therefore our hope is in You,
for You are the one who does all this.

JEREMIAH 14:22

God is our only hope in every situation. When we feel utterly helpless, depend on God and He will bring you through every trial. If God is our only hope then we need to be prepared and have enough faith to wait for the Lord to take action.

If you are suffering as a result of sin, like the people of Judah in today's Scripture verse, then confess it. Sin brings only pain and suffering, but God brings redemption. Confess your sin to Him and take comfort in the incredible, undeserved grace that God offers.

Holy God, I confess my sins with deep remorse and know that You will not cast me away, but will embrace me with forgiveness. Amen.

Experience God's Faithful Love

You forgave the iniquity of Your people and covered all their sins. You set aside all Your wrath and turned from Your fierce anger. Will you not revive us again, that Your people may rejoice in You?

PSALM 85:2–3, 6

It has become common nowadays to deny sin and its consequences, but there are millions of people who live under the burden of their sin.

God's grace gives our lives new meaning, leading us to a new and more productive life. His grace allows us to move in a new direction once our sins have been forgiven.

If we just confess our sin and ask for forgiveness then God is merciful and will forgive us. Think of all that He has already forgiven and give Him praise.

I thank and praise You, Lord, my God, that in Your mercy You have forgiven all my sins and helped me to bear fruit to Your glory. Amen.

Christ Understands

Because He Himself suffered when He was tempted,
He is able to help those who are being tempted.

HEBREWS 2:18

Because the Lord Jesus was totally human, He experienced temptation and trials in the same way that we do. The difference is that He triumphed over every hardship to fulfill His task of salvation for us.

He understands our temptations, trials, and human weaknesses. If you ever feel like a failure, don't despair! Remember that Jesus will restore your courage with His love and understanding. He understands us and knows what is best for each one of us at all times. He is not only our Savior, but also our Friend.

The wonder of God's grace is that Christ not only understands our needs, He also intercedes for us with the Father so that our faith may endure.

*Thank You, Lord Jesus, for Your love
and understanding, and the restorative
power of Your endless grace. Amen.*

God's Grace-Filled Love

May the Lord direct your hearts into
God's love and Christ's perseverance.

2 THESSALONIANS 3:5

We cherish in our hearts the eternal truth that God's love is free and undeserved. Nothing that you have done or intend to do can earn you that.

God loves you because God is love, and this is a great truth for which we are eternally grateful and for which we should glorify and thank Him.

You are the object of God's love. God Himself lit the flame of love for Him in your heart, so you must do all you can to ensure that nothing extinguishes this inner flame inside you.

Truly, You are love! Your Son became
man to demonstrate true love, Father.
Help me to radiate love in return. Amen.

The Man of Sorrows

He was despised and rejected by men,
a Man of sorrows, and familiar with suffering.

ISAIAH 53:3

Christ's suffering was unique and stands out in world history. It emerges from the plains of time as a monument of remembrance to the Man of sorrows' suffering – for you and me. It reminds us that God's grace does not come cheap: the price was suffering, sorrow and blood; the blood of His only Son who became human for our sake.

Jesus, the One without sin, in obedience to the Father, became sin for our sakes. The unbearable burden of the sins of all people through the ages was placed on His shoulders and He vicariously carried it to Golgotha.

Lord Jesus, it was for me that You had to endure
scorn and suffering, for me that You had to be
crucified. Thank You, Jesus, that You died for me
so that I may inherit everlasting life. Amen.

Seek to Please God

*For they loved praise from men
more than praise from God.*

JOHN 12:43

The only way to achieve the very best in life, and to develop the feeling of self-confidence and fulfillment that is so essential to your peace of mind, is to stay true in all things to your high calling in Jesus.

He is constant – yesterday, today and for all eternity. He will never forsake you or fail you. Place your full trust in Him and not in fallible people. You will never be disappointed.

*We do not understand it, Lord, but Your way
is always best. You will never forsake us
and we know that we are safe in You. Amen.*

Remember God's Share in Your Success

By the grace of God I am what I am, and His grace to me was not without effect.

1 CORINTHIANS 15:10

There are many people who declare that they are "self-made people" and that their success is solely through their own doing.

It is a foolish person indeed who convinces himself that the honor for his accomplishments is his alone. Everyone faces problems and stumbling blocks in their careers. If God's hand of grace was not shielding you, you would never have triumphed over your problems and adversities.

By gratefully acknowledging God in your achievements, and by thanking Him for His grace and goodness, an extra dimension of joy and happiness that you have not yet experienced will be added to your life.

Thank You for blessing us so undeservedly and so abundantly, Lord. You are our salvation and courage for each day. Amen.

When God Lives in You

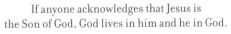

If anyone acknowledges that Jesus is
the Son of God, God lives in him and he in God.

1 JOHN 4:15

The simple teachings of Jesus Christ have enormous power and if you embrace God, you will have a force in your life like you have never experienced before.

The miraculous truth is that you will not live alone with God, but He will live in you. This is the most amazing and significant experience that you will ever witness; your disposition towards people and circumstances changes; you notice the beauty of life instead of focusing on its dreariness; your objectives are creative and you work positively toward them.

Acknowledging Christ results in such far-reaching consequences that you will stand in wonder each day at what God has achieved in your life through His grace.

*I wish to celebrate Your strength. Make me
victorious in battle through Your Spirit. Amen.*

Inconceivable Grace

"So is My word that goes out from My mouth:
It will not return to Me empty, but will accomplish what
I desire and achieve the purpose for which I sent it."

ISAIAH 55:11

Lord, my God, I glorify and praise Your holy name. Your love knows no boundaries! I thank You that I have meditated on Your promises; may Your precious words become part of my thoughts, life and conduct.

Stand by me through the Holy Spirit so that I will always have a warm heart for others, so that I may perform the true service of love, in Your name and to Your glory. In this way I will not fail to find Your mercy.

Let me never forget how dependent I am on You. I will always hold firmly onto Your hand and so inherit Your kingdom.

Lord, soften my heart to others so I may glorify Your name. I ask for all this through the blood of Jesus, my Savior and Redeemer. Amen.

Now and Then

Now we see but a poor reflection as in a mirror;
then we shall see face to face.

1 CORINTHIANS 13:12

"Now" and "then" are two little words with profound meaning. While we are in this life "now" we have to contend with many situations that look dark and problematic.

But how blessed and happy we will be when we remember both sides of His promise: "now" is a mirror and a poor reflection, but "then" I will see all the glory that God has prepared for His children.

One day we will come face-to-face with our Lord, and only then will we discover how often His love and grace shielded us from disasters and dangers.

*I thank You, my Lord, that Your love and grace guide
me from day to day. With this blessed assurance
I praise and glorify You all my life. Amen.*

Provider of Needs

God is able to make all grace abound to you,
so that in all things at all times, having all that
you need, you will abound in every good work.

2 CORINTHIANS 9:8

God loves the generous giver and blesses him. God Himself gives abundantly so that His children may have enough in all things. He gave His Son, the Holy Spirit, and the excitement of a new, redeemed life. God promises us that we will have all that we need.

If we trust in the Lord completely, we can be certain, regardless of how dark the storm clouds are above us, how great the need – we will always have sufficient strength and grace; we only need to ask God to provide in our need.

From His unfathomable grace, He will every day, in every way, provide in all our needs through life. His love knows no bounds!

Thank You for the quiet assurance, Lord Jesus,
that I will always have sufficient strength and
grace for every situation in life. Amen.

Your Spiritual Reserves

I pray that out of His glorious riches He may strengthen
you with power through His Spirit in your inner being.

EPHESIANS 3:16

If our lives are to have true meaning, they must have depth. To live a superficial life is to develop a poor, ineffective lifestyle. To live profoundly requires a certainty about the Holy Spirit's ability to work in and through you.

Realizing that the Holy Spirit expresses Himself through people, you begin to fathom the immense potential in your life. The spiritual reserves that are available to you come from God and can never be exhausted. All the measures of God's grace are available to you and are ready to be used.

To be able to draw from these gifts of grace, it is imperative to spend much time and energy pursuing them.

O Spirit of God, lead me into the depths of spiritual
growth and strengthen my faith and love daily. Amen.

The Feast of God's Grace

The angel said to her, "Do not be afraid,
Mary, you have found favor with God."

LUKE 1:30

God is no respecter of persons – all people are equal before Him. God has no favorites.

Through the responsibility placed on her, Mary revealed the quality of her life and her devotion to the heavenly Father. As far as it is known, she led a quiet life somewhere in the hills of Judea, unknown except to her family. And yet she was chosen above all women as God's instrument through which He would reveal Himself to the world.

Your love for and devotion to God may seem unimportant, but if you offer Him your very best, He will use you in His own unique way. Then you will experience the feast of God's grace.

I praise and thank You, Father, that You reveal
Yourself time and again to me. Use me as an instrument
to spread Your love through the world. Amen.

december

JOY IN GOD

The Joy of Life in Christ

"Blessed rather are those who hear
the word of God and obey it."

LUKE 11:28

Many people regard the observing of religious principles as a tiresome yet necessary discipline. Christians should have a more positive attitude to their faith because Jesus came so that we could have life in all its abundance. He wants our lives to be filled with purpose, vitality and joy.

The basis of our Christian experience is a relationship with our caring heavenly Father who wants only the best for His children. What more could anyone ask of life? Here you have the promise of the very best that life can offer, and all that God expects of you is to yield to His sovereignty in your life. This is not a lot to ask for when you consider what you are getting in exchange; a life of fulfillment and joy.

Lord, I rejoice in the knowledge that You redeemed me and have given me a life of joy and fulfillment. Amen.

Jesus, the Source of All True Happiness

Hosanna! Blessed is He who comes in the name of the Lord! Blessed is the coming kingdom of our father David!

MARK 11:9-10

To be blessed we must know Jesus as our personal Savior and Redeemer; we must commit our lives to Him and be obedient to His will.

We all search for happiness, on our own terms, and because of this we run the risk of missing Christ's blessing. Man's happiness often depends on chance or luck: a sudden change in our condition. It is something that life offers and then, just as suddenly, rips away.

Man calls it happiness when things go his way for a while, but Christ's happiness is a happiness that is different; it is a joy in Him.

Lord Jesus, I praise Your glorious name for You are the source of all my happiness because You delivered me and made me a child of God. Amen.

Let Love Inspire Service

Blessed is the King who comes in the name of the Lord!
Peace in heaven and glory in the highest!

LUKE 19:38

When we read the account of Jesus' triumphant entry into Jerusalem, we cannot help but feel the joy and excitement of those who offered Him such a sincere welcome. Throughout the ages this same feeling of wonderment, awe and joy has been experienced by people who welcomed Christ into their lives.

Jesus said that He came so that you may experience the fullness of life (see John 10:10). This means that you can live in peace and calm in the certain knowledge that He is with you at all times.

Welcome the Master into your life with the same joy as the people of Jerusalem did and experience the joy that Christ brings.

Redeemer and Friend, in love and compassion,
by Your grace You raise me from sin and shame,
so that I may be Your joyful child. Amen.

Joyous Assurance!

"Take courage! It is I. Don't be afraid."

MATTHEW 14:27

Many of God's children have forgotten how to live with joy and peace. They identify with the spirit of the day and forget that, as Christians, they have the ability to rise above the turmoil of our times.

Christian joy is not a giddy emotion that ignores evil or shrugs it off. Christ *commands* His disciples to remain cheerful and courageous. This implies that they should be aware of the worst that can happen and yet, with Christian optimism, hope for the best.

Even when you are afraid and despair stalks you, hold steadfastly to the truth that God is always in control. Christians should be joyful and at peace because they have a living hope in their hearts.

Mighty Redeemer, through Your indwelling Spirit I can face the future with joy and peace of mind. Amen.

Awake, My Soul!

*"Our friend Lazarus has fallen asleep;
but I am going there to wake him up."*

JOHN 11:11

How appropriate Jesus' words are for us today!
There are many people who need to be woken
from their indifference, their hopelessness, and
their helplessness.

They forget that, in the midst of all the problems in the world today, it is not only important, but also imperative that your whole life
should be grounded on your faith in the living
Christ.

Just as Jesus raised Lazarus from the dead,
so will He raise you from your spiritual stupor
and inspire you to live a life of victory, joy and
success in His service.

*Lord Jesus, I worship You as the Lord and Savior
of my life, and commit myself anew to living
according to Your ways. Amen.*

Indestructible Joy

Rejoice in the Lord always. I will say it again: Rejoice!
Let your gentleness be evident to all. The Lord is near.

PHILIPPIANS 4:4–5

Many people think we simply have to endure this life so that we can go to heaven one day. If, however, we do not practice the art of cheerfulness now, we will not appreciate the joy in heaven. That is why we, the redeemed, should become part of God's feast here and now.

We do accept that our sins are forgiven, but refuse to express our joy daily. We cautiously and longingly remain on the edge of receiving invincible Christian joy, thus robbing ourselves and others of one of God's greatest gifts.

The Christian's joy is in Christ Jesus. In Him God came very near to us. Christ met God's demands and filled our lives with joy. Therefore, our joy should be unceasing and everlasting, because Christ is its Source.

*Jesus, Joy of our lives, we want to rejoice in You
now already, in preparation for heaven. Amen.*

Your Salvation Is Here!

*The LORD has made proclamation to the ends
of the earth: "Say to the Daughter of Zion,
'See, your Savior comes!'"*

ISAIAH 62:11

At Christmas we commemorate the coming of Christ into the world, but we must never forget about the coming of Christ into our hearts.

If we want to experience the real joy of Christmas, Christ has to pour out His salvation and peace into our hearts. Thank God that Christ not only came into the world, but also personally comes into the hearts of those who believe in Him. He came to find and redeem those who were lost.

He comes to you today with His hands filled with grace and forgiveness and blessings; He comes to turn your sadness into joy.

*Jesus, my Savior and Redeemer, thank You that
I can experience the all-surpassing joy and
happiness of one who has been redeemed. Amen.*

An Amazing Truth

*I pray that you … may have power, together
with all the saints, to grasp how wide and
long and high and deep is the love of Christ.*

EPHESIANS 3:17-18

When you become so aware of the presence
of God's love that you no longer doubt His
existence, your spirit experiences the liberating
assurance that God really exists.

The awesome wonder is that you not only
love Him, but that He loves you; you belong to
Him and He is in control of your life.

Ordinary people like us may know God personally, and He knows us – this is the amazing
truth and good news of Christianity. Christ
taught us that as He is one with the Father, His
disciples can live in unity with Him in the same
way (see John 17:22-23). Those who accept and
love Christ share in His unique relationship
with God.

*O Lord, let me live in close union
with You, the True Vine. Amen.*

True Holiness

"My thoughts are not your thoughts, neither are your ways My ways," declares the Lord.

ISAIAH 55:8

To many people it seems inconceivable that a life of fullness and great joy can be likened to holiness. Yet true holiness is the most dynamic, creative and meaningful lifestyle in the world.

To be holy implies that you live in a right relationship with God. It causes you to enjoy life to the full and also gives you a greater understanding of people.

The secret of a balanced, joyful, rewarding life is to live in such a way that it is easy for the Lord to reveal Himself through you. This is the way of true sanctification, but is also the road to a successful life according to God's standard.

Teach me, O Holy Spirit, the true meaning of holiness and enable me to live a life that will bring glory and honor to You each day. Amen.

Christ Is Coming Again!

You ought to live holy and godly lives as you look forward to the day of God and speed its coming.

2 PETER 3:11-12

During His life on earth Jesus was often asked when exactly God's kingdom would come? His reply was always the same, "No one knows about that day or hour, not even the angels in heaven, nor the Son, but only the Father" (Matt. 24:36). Christ, however, emphasized that His followers had to be prepared for it at all times.

Your only concern as a Christian should be to ensure that you live your daily life in accordance with the pattern that God has set before you. You must obey His commands in love; pray zealously; continually praise and worship Him; and also study His Word.

Then you will be fully equipped to eagerly await His return and, when He comes in glory, to receive Him with joy and gladness.

Lord, help me to be ready when You return.
Let me work to the glory of Your
name in the meantime. Amen.

The Joy of Faith

He who unites himself with the
Lord is one with Him in spirit.

1 CORINTHIANS 6:17

Joy and gladness are not the main goals of the Christian faith, but important by-products of it. The focus and purpose of our faith is the Lord Himself. When His life-giving Spirit fills your heart, the joy of a Christ-filled life becomes yours.

Forgiveness and a Spirit-filled life bring great joy to all who strive to live in Christ. And the culmination of this joy is to live in the constant awareness of the presence of God. You find yourself in fellowship with Him at all times, in all places. The more you become aware of His closeness, the stronger and more meaningful your faith gets. Then joy, unspeakable and full of glory, will flow from you.

Father, I want to express my gratitude to
You for Your closeness by living a life that
glorifies You in every way. Amen.

Our Calling to Cheerfulness

Rejoice in the Lord always. I will say it again: Rejoice!

PHILIPPIANS 4:4

Christians are supposed to rejoice, and if joy fills our lives, we will reap rich rewards spiritually. Many people spread gloom and doom wherever they go, but as a child of God, you can spread joy and inspiration because Christ has given us an indestructible joy that carries us through life.

When you are spiritually sensitive, you have no reason to be despondent. Your daily walk with Jesus Christ, the glorious promises in His Word and God's profound mercy will fill your life with joy, purpose and direction.

Your cheerfulness is not a façade that you put up to impress people but comes from a heart and mind that are in harmony with God through Jesus Christ.

Lord, You fill my days with joy. Your peace flows through me like a quiet stream. Amen.

Happiness in Christ

*He who has clean hands and a pure heart, who does
not lift up his soul to an idol or swear by what
is false. He will receive blessings from the
Lord and vindication from God his Savior.*

PSALM 24:4–5

No one can take away the joy and blessings that
Christ gives us. We can find joy in Christ even
when we are in pain. This joy cannot be erased
by sorrow, loss, disappointment, or failure. It is
a happiness that sees a rainbow through tears.

The joy that is found in Christ does not depend on our circumstances. It is a deep, everlasting and steadfast joy. It is not something
that we can strive for and attain through any
human endeavor. It is a gift of God's grace.

The Holy Spirit will strengthen and guide
us to obey Christ, so that His happiness and
blessing will become our portion.

*Loving Master, thank You that the joy You give is
steadfast and indestructible – unlike the temporary
and transient happiness of the world. Amen.*

Christmas: Feast of the Child

She gave birth to her firstborn, a Son. She wrapped Him in cloths and placed Him in a manger, because there was no room for them in the inn.

LUKE 2:7

Every Christmas we become children at heart again. For a short time we leave our mundane lives and wander down the paths of rich imagination, of wonder and delightful joy, while we freely rejoice in the infinite love of God.

Even the staunchest realist finds his heart stirred when he hears the age-old story of God's love.

As we experience the mystery of Christmas both tangibly and intangibly, we are touched by the wonder of God's love – and our dreams of peace and joy are rekindled.

I thank You, Lord Jesus, that I can enjoy the festivities surrounding Christmas with childlike glee and so enter into Your kingdom as a little child. Amen.

The Omnipresent Christ

Jesus Christ is the same yesterday and today and forever.

HEBREWS 13:8

The living Christ is the Eternal Being who came to earth to reveal God in human form. This amazing truth is actually too sublime for the human mind to grasp. It would have remained this way if it had not been for Christ's wonderful simplicity.

Jesus did not make His entry into this world accompanied by hosts of angels – no, He was a baby in a manger. He became a carpenter who made friends with fishermen and tax collectors. Yet His eternal nature is not obscure to the sensitive follower who is willing to accept His divine authority. And as He was with those people in His eternal image, so He is with you today. This is a source of great comfort.

Jesus Christ is still the same, loving, healing, helping Lord, who gives Himself to all who seek Him and love Him.

Omnipresent Savior, I praise You for Your Spirit that dwells in me to teach, guide and comfort me. Amen.

Can You Truly Celebrate Christmas?

Then they opened their treasures and presented Him with gifts of gold and of incense and of myrrh.

MATTHEW 2:11

The Magi understood the true meaning behind Christmas – to give. At Christmas, God gave His best, His most valuable treasure – His Son. And the Child of Bethlehem also gave – He gave Himself in His death on the cross.

Learn the secret of giving from giving. Forget what you did for others and remember what others have done for you. Rather than expecting things from others, ask what you can do for them. Look around you to see where you can sow seeds of joy and kindness and love.

If you are willing to do these things, then you will have brought your offering of gold, frankincense and myrrh to the Lord. And you will experience the true joy of Christmas.

Generous Lord, this Christmas season I once again offer my life to You to do as You please. Amen.

Take a Break

"In repentance and rest is your salvation,
in quietness and trust is your strength,
but you would have none of it."

ISAIAH 30:15

As we withdraw from the confusion of daily life over Christmastime and spend more time in nature, we once again connect with God. Slow down and enjoy the things that we let slip in the everyday rush of the rest of the year: long conversations with family members; the beauty of creation; the delight in a child's eyes; playing with pets; and most of all, digging deep into the Word of God.

Look up into the branches of tall trees, and remember that they grow slowly. Allow God to bring His refreshing strength into your life again, and accept His gifts of peace and joy.

Creator God, thank You for restoring Your peace and
joy to me in times of quietness and rest. Amen.

Fulfillment in Christ

As the deer pants for streams of water,
so my soul pants for You, O God.
My soul thirsts for God, for the living God.

PSALM 42:1–2

The same longing that moved the psalmist's heart is evident in the hearts of people today. Although they desire to know God, they wander blindly along paths that do not lead to Him, finding no joy or satisfaction.

However, those who are truly wise know that true satisfaction and fulfillment are to be found only in spiritual things. A proper balance between material and spiritual aspects of life must be maintained; and this is only possible when Christ is at the center of your life.

The Lord cares about every aspect of your life, and when you taste and see that He is good, your life will be rich and fruitful.

Living Savior, in You alone I find fulfillment and satisfaction. Praise Your holy name. Amen.

Christ-Feast!

*Do not be afraid. I bring you good news of
great joy that will be for all the people.*

LUKE 2:10

The world has eliminated Christ from the festivities of Christmas to make room for worldly
pleasures. As Christians we need to rectify this
travesty.

Christmas must not be allowed to degen-
erate into cheap tinsel, shining lights and superficial emotions. We must look beneath the
trappings and uncover the core of Christmas,
letting the Light of the world shine in our lives.

Christians have more reason to celebrate
Christmas than others do. The true glory of
Christmas is to be found in our hearts – not in
the malls or at parties. Let the world see in us
the true spirit of Christmas so that they too can
come and worship the King.

*Holy Spirit of God, this Christmas guide me
past the external trappings to the true inner joy
that can only be found in Christ. Amen.*

Festive Season of the Soul

Today in the town of David a Savior has
been born to you; He is Christ the Lord.

LUKE 2:11

The world is filled with the sounds of Christmas.
You can hear festive songs, bells and laughter.
And if you listen with your soul, you will hear
the angels singing, the joy of anticipation and
the sanctified sound of holy silence. You will
hear the whisper of the eternal Word that became flesh in Jesus Christ.

Christmas is a continuous season of the soul,
and Bethlehem lives forever in your heart.
Through God's grace, the eyes and ears of your
heart will be opened and you will hear the joyful sounds of celebration because of the Word
that came to live among us.

Savior and Friend of sinners, thank You for
this season of the soul when we can listen to
the soundless Word that became flesh. Amen.

A Star Shines in Bethlehem

When they saw the star, they were overjoyed.

MATTHEW 2:10

Christmas brings a feeling of joy, goodwill and peace to our hearts. Jesus came to bring light to this dark world.

The light of the star guided people to the manger so that they could joyfully behold their Savior. The Star of Bethlehem still lights your path through the darkness of temptation and wickedness to bring you to the path that leads to God.

During this festive season, and as you approach the new year, fix your eyes upon the Savior of the world. He is your Guiding Star and will lead you to joy, peace and goodwill.

Guiding Star, thank You for leading me along the path that leads to eternal life. Amen.

Christ Is Born!

*Jesus was born in Bethlehem in Judea,
during the time of King Herod.*

MATTHEW 2:1

It is an irrefutable historical fact that Jesus was born in Bethlehem. Through this physical birth, God revealed Himself to all of humanity.

In spite of the world's festivities around Christmastime, if you have not experienced the birth of Christ in your heart, you will never know the true joy and peace of Christmas.

If you want to experience true Christmas joy, Christ must be living in your heart and be given the place of honor in your life – the very center of it. When His holiness permeates your life, it becomes a "merry Christmas" in the truest sense of the word.

I thank You, holy Child of Bethlehem, for being born in me so that I can partake of Your Spirit, and so that my entire life can be a celebration in Your honor. Amen.

Worship God with Gladness

Shout for joy to the LORD, all the earth.
Worship the LORD with gladness;
come before Him with joyful songs.

PSALM 100:1-2

During this festive season, let's remember to have heartfelt joy in everything that God has given us and for all that He has done for us. Let our praises to God be like beautiful harmonious music that rises up to Him.

God delights in the joy of His people who are thankful for what He has given them.

Joy, happiness and excitement are often associated with earthly pleasures, but we should learn to associate these feelings with worshiping God and having knowledge of His ways.

As we draw nearer to Christmas, thank God for His goodness, delight yourself in all that He has given you, and share that joy with everybody you come into contact with.

Holy God, I come before You with utterances of holy joy. Help me to share my joy with others. Amen.

Feast of Hope

Always be prepared to give an answer to everyone who asks you to give the reason for the hope that you have.

1 PETER 3:15

With the state of today's world, it would be easy to give up hope, but as the year draws to a close, the blessed Feast of Christ comes to remind us that Jesus came to this world to save sinners.

Regardless of the despondency and despair surrounding us, a beacon of love is shining – the Light of the world – who invites us to leave the darkness behind, put our hope in Him and face the future with expectation and joy.

Advent should remind us time and again that, even if we suffer, Christ is still our hope for the future; as He has been for His children through the ages.

Lord Jesus of Bethlehem, thank You that You came to place hope in our hearts and our lives. Amen.

Serve Christ Joyfully

"If you love Me, you will obey what I command."
JOHN 14:15

Many people regard their surrender to Christ as a strict discipline that adds an unbearable burden on their lives. They consequently lead an unsatisfying spiritual life.

Your life in Christ should be joyful, and as you grow in Christ, your joy should increase. If you are truly devoted to Christ, your highest desire will be to get to know Him better and serve Him more effectively.

To reach this point in your pilgrimage, you have to get to know Him increasingly better through Bible study. However, you also have to know the living Christ personally by talking with Him in prayer. Strive to be with Christ, and the more He becomes an inseparable part of your life, the more joy you will experience.

I rejoice in Your service, O Lord.
Thank You for this wonderful privilege. Amen.

Continue to Praise and Thank God

The shepherds returned, glorifying and praising God for all the things they had heard and seen.

LUKE 2:20

The festivities are over: the wilted Christmas tree is out the back door, the glossy paper is crumpled, and party hats lie neglected in a corner. The excitement and joy that most people associate with Christmas is now a thing of the past and everybody returns to the routine of daily life.

But this should not be the case! The joyous event that we celebrate on Christ's birthday does not begin and end there. Certainly Christmas is a day of celebration when we attempt to thank God for the gift of His Son, but today and every other day should be reason enough for us to be joyful and praise Christ for His constant presence.

Thank You, Lord Jesus, for yet another Christmas. May every day of our lives be a feast of Christ. Amen.

Serve the Lord Joyously

The joy of the LORD is your strength.

NEHEMIAH 8:10

There are times in our lives, especially when the festivities of the season are winding down, when we feel powerless and grief seems to take hold of our hearts.

Note that our verse today does not state that our joy lies in our own strength. Rather, it says that we have the Lord's joy. What could be better than that?

Our feelings are uncertain and unstable, but the Lord never changes. He is always there, but we must not allow clouds of uncertainty to hide His face. It is a precious assurance for every believer – I serve the Lord joyously and He shelters me.

Please, Lord Jesus, let me serve You with happiness and joy and, in so doing, become a powerful testimony of You in this dismal world. Amen.

Everlasting Joy

"No one will take away your joy."

JOHN 16:22

The world's joy is temporary and transitory, but Christ's joy is a deep well of quiet happiness – stable and steadfast.

In the eyes of the world, it may seem unnatural to have joy in certain situations, but with Christ's peace that fills and encircles our lives, we may rest assured that His eternal fountain of inner joy is guaranteed and no one can take it away.

Therefore I can rejoice because everlasting joy is mine. My Savior promises it. I rest cheerfully in Him because He will see to it that no evil power will rob me of my joy.

Holy Spirit of God, thank You that one of Your gifts is joy. Let me never disappoint my Lord by being a despondent Christian. Amen.

Joy in the Lord

"Whoever wants to save his life will lose it,
but whoever loses his life for Me will find it."

MATTHEW 16:25

Strange as it may sound, most people feel worship is a burden and not a joy. They feel that they have to lay down so many things that are precious to them and enter into a life of seriousness and hardship. They forget the fact that when God asks us to lay down our old life, we can be confident that He will replace it with something much better.

Don't believe for one moment that when God requires total obedience from you, that your life will lose its joy and gladness. If He calls you to obedience, trust Him completely. He promised to bear our burdens. Rejoice in the Lord and in His omnipotence and accept your duty with gladness and gratitude.

I want to accept my task with gladness,
Lord, because I know that with Your help it
will never be too burdensome for me. Amen.

Joy in God's Presence

How lovely is Your dwelling place, O Lord
Almighty! My soul yearns, even faints, for the
courts of the Lord. Blessed are those who dwell
in Your house; they are ever praising You.

PSALM 84:1–2, 4

Far too often we envy people because they have
things that we lack. We forget that material
things do not determine our joy and that they
can never give true satisfaction and contentment. Only a healthy relationship with God
can ensure that you will have eternal joy.

Praise God for the blessings that He gives
His faithful children: grace, protection, prosperity, honor and joy. God will not withhold
any good thing from those who are obedient to
Him. He will supply all your needs out of the
riches of His grace. Give Him thanks for His
goodness and bountiful grace.

*Lord God, I praise You because You have so generously
loaded me with blessings and all good things. Amen.*

Celebration

*"Do wedding guests fast while celebrating
with the groom? Of course not. They
can't fast while the groom is with them."*

MARK 2:19 (NLT)

In this Scripture, Jesus portrays Himself as the groom at a wedding and His followers as the groom's guests.

Their weddings were not the half-day celebrations we know today, but often lasted a whole week. With this, Christ was pronouncing a loud and clear "no" to everyone who wanted to turn religion into a long-faced, joyless endurance test. He was saying, "To live with Me is to celebrate life!"

Celebrating life with Jesus is experiencing life with all its joys and sorrows, successes and failures with a cheerful heart and attitude. It is to hope against hope, and to seek the lovely, the good and the holy.

*Father God, turn all our sorrow
into pure joy in You. Amen.*